Workbook 4

Caribbean Primary Social Studies
Our World Community

LISA GREENSTEIN

HODDER EDUCATION
AN HACHETTE UK COMPANY

Acknowledgements

The Publisher expresses gratitude to Ms Jeannelle Antoine-Thomas for her assistance and guidance in the preparation of this book.

The Publishers would like to thank the following for permission to reproduce copyright material:

Photo acknowledgements
p. 4 *cc* © Vilna Robotav 3d/Adobe Stock Photo; **p. 19** *br* © Janusz Pieńkowski/Alamy Stock Photo; **p. 20** *br* © Historic Images/Alamy Stock Photo; **p. 22** *tr* © Glasshouse Images/Alamy Stock Photo; **p. 28** *cr* © 506 Collection/Alamy Stock Photo; **p. 35** *bl* © AS Photo Project/Adobe Stock Photo; **p. 35** *bc* © Hamzeh/Adobe Stock Photo; **p. 35** *bc* © Hamzeh/Adobe Stock Photo; **p. 35** *bc* © Hamzeh/Adobe Stock Photo; **p. 35** *bc* © Hamzeh/Adobe Stock Photo; **p. 35** *br* © Hamzeh/Adobe Stock Photo; **p. 60** *tl* © Oleksandr Kharchenko/Alamy Stock Photo; **p. 60** *tr, tc, tc* © Dzmitry Kliapitski/Alamy Stock Photo; **p. 69** *tl* © Aksinia/Adobe Stock Photo; **p. 69** *tr* © Light Field Studios/Adobe Stock Photo; **p. 69** *cl* © Nomad Soul/Adobe Stock Photo; **p. 69** *cr* © DC Studio/Adobe Stock Photo; **p. 69** *bl* © Maroke/Adobe Stock Photo; **p. 69** *br* © Moodboard/Adobe Stock Photo; **p. 71** *cl* © Rogatnev/Adobe Stock Photo; **p. 71** *cc* © Katsiaryna/Adobe Stock Photo; **p. 71** *cc* © Mary San/Adobe Stock Photo; **p. 71** *cc* © Sashkin/Adobe Stock Photo; **p. 71** *cc* © Rnko/Adobe Stock Photo; **p. 71** *cr* © Macro Vector/Adobe Stock Photo; **p. 71** *cc* © Francois Poirier/Adobe Stock Photo; **p. 71** *cc* © GR Group/Adobe Stock Photo; **p. 71** *cc* © Aleksangel/Adobe Stock Photo; **p. 71** *cl* © Sonulkaster/Adobe Stock Photo; **p. 71** *cc* © Francois Poirier/Adobe Stock Photo; **p. 71** *bc* © Olga Sh/Adobe Stock Photo; **p. 71** *bc* © Begun 1983/Adobe Stock Photo; **p. 85** *tr* © Moonrun/Adobe Stock Photo.

t = top, *b* = bottom, *l* = left, *r* = right, *c* = centre

Every effort has been made to trace all copyright holders, but if any have been inadvertently overlooked, the Publishers will be pleased to make the necessary arrangements at the first opportunity.

Although every effort has been made to ensure that website addresses are correct at time of going to press, Hodder Education cannot be held responsible for the content of any website mentioned in this book. It is sometimes possible to find a relocated web page by typing in the address of the home page for a website in the URL window of your browser.

Hachette UK's policy is to use papers that are natural, renewable and recyclable products and made from wood grown in well-managed forests and other controlled sources. The logging and manufacturing processes are expected to conform to the environmental regulations of the country of origin.

Orders: please contact Hachette UK Distribution, Hely Hutchinson Centre, Milton Road, Didcot, Oxfordshire, OX11 7HH. Telephone: +44 (0)1235 827827. Email education@hachette.co.uk Lines are open from 9 a.m. to 5 p.m., Monday to Friday. You can also order through our website: www.hoddereducation.com

ISBN: 9781510480759

© Lisa Greenstein 2021

First published in 2021 by

Hodder Education (a trading division of Hodder & Stoughton Limited),

An Hachette UK Company

Carmelite House

50 Victoria Embankment

London EC4Y 0DZ

www.hoddereducation.com

The authorised representative in the EEA is Hachette Ireland, 8 Castlecourt Centre, Dublin 15, D15 XTP3, Ireland (email: info@hbgi.ie)

Impression number   10 9 8 7 6 5 4 3

Year   2025

All rights reserved. Apart from any use permitted under UK copyright law, no part of this publication may be reproduced or transmitted in any form or by any means, electronic or mechanical, including photocopying and recording, or held within any information storage and retrieval system, without permission in writing from the publisher or under licence from the Copyright Licensing Agency Limited. Further details of such licences (for reprographic reproduction) may be obtained from the Copyright Licensing Agency Limited, www.cla.co.uk

Cover by Marc Monés from Davila Illustration Agency

Illustrations by Vian Oelofsen and Stéphan Theron

Typeset in FS Albert 12/16 by IO Publishing CC

Printed by Ashford Colour Ltd

A catalogue record for this title is available from the British Library.

Contents

	How to use this book	4
1	Belonging to a family	5
2	Our groups	8
Revise and prepare		12
3	Locating my community	14
4	Heritage	18
5	Caribbean groupings	28
Revise and prepare		33
6	National identity	35
7	Travel and migration	39
8	Human rights	42
9	The justice system	47
Revise and prepare		51
10	You can depend on me	52
11	Caring for each other	54
Revise and prepare		57
12	Telecommunication	58
13	Communicating in our region	62
Revise and prepare		66
14	Human resources	67
15	Goods and services	71
Revise and prepare		78
16	Damage to the environment	79
17	Improving quality of life	81
Revise and prepare		83
CPEA Practice Questions		84

How to use this book

Welcome to Caribbean Primary Social Studies Workbook 4. This workbook aims to prepare you for the Caribbean Primary Exit Assessment (CPEA) or any similar assessments.

As you work through each chapter in the book, complete as many of the activities and exercises as you can. There may be some information that you do not know. This means you need to do some research. Research means working to find out information. You can do research in different ways:

- Visit a library, and look up the information in books.
- Ask questions to members of your family and your community.
- Do internet searches, and find websites with more information.
- Think of places where the information might be available, for example a business or a tourist information centre.
- Observe people, things and activities around you.

You will also find sections in this book called 'Revise and prepare'. These sections aim to prepare you for the CPEA at the end of Grade 6. You can prepare by completing the assignments and tests in these sections. Your teacher or parent can help you check your work against the answers online at www.hoddereducation.co.uk/caribbean-primary-social-studies

1 Belonging to a family

Different kinds of families

There are different types of families.

nuclear family

single-parent family

extended family

1. Talk about:
   a. the characteristics of each type of family
   b. the type of family you prefer
   c. why you prefer this type of family
   d. the difficulties and challenges of living in each type of family structure
   e. the reasons why there are so many different types of families.

2. Write your own definitions here.

   key words

   nuclear family ....
   single-parent family ....
   extended family ....

3. If Sandy lives in a nuclear family, she lives with _____. (Choose the correct letter.)
   a. her mum, dad and siblings
   b. her mum and siblings
   c. her grandparents, dad and cousins

4. Study the pictures of types of families, and tick (✔) the one that shows an extended family.

5

Unit 1 Belonging to a family

My place in the family

Brothers and sisters are called **siblings**. In a family, the older siblings need to be **role models** for younger children. As you get older, you develop more **maturity**. Maturity means growing up physically as well as becoming more understanding of others and more responsible.

1. What do you understand by the term 'role model'?

2. Identify two things that the older children are doing in the pictures to serve as role models for their younger siblings.

3. Sometimes in a family, people act in ways that do not contribute to cooperation and peace. This results in conflict. When this happens, other family members need to behave in a mature and responsible way for the good of the family. Brainstorm and discuss actions that do and do not contribute to cooperation among family members.

Decision-making

> **Decision-making** is the process of making choices, or deciding what to do. In many families, the adults discuss and make decisions together. Sometimes, children are also involved in decision-making.

1 Who makes decisions in your family? Are you involved? Write about how your family usually makes decisions.

_____
_____
_____

2 In the grey blocks, write the names of people in your family.

For each decision, tick (✔) one or more people who would make or help to make the decision.

In the extra rows, fill in any other decisions that families need to make, and tick (✔) to show who makes or helps to make this decision in your family.

What we need to decide	Who decides				
Where we live					
What we are having for dinner					
What to do during the holidays					
Who does which chores					
Which sports and activities I do					
What time I go to bed					
What I can wear					

3 Do you think it is important to consider everyone's views in a family? Should some members of the family have more say than others? Explain your views.

_____
_____
_____
_____
_____

2 Our groups

Moving into adolescence

Adolescence – also called the **teenage** years – is the stage of development from 13 to 19 years, when you change and mature from a child to an adult. The years just before this are known as pre-adolescence, also called the '**tween**' or '**preteen**' years. Between the ages of 9 and 12, even before your body starts maturing, you may begin to change in how you think and feel, especially your sense of **identity** – your sense of who you are.

* Your **self-identity** is how you see yourself, your likes and dislikes, and all the things that are unique about you.
* Your **social identity** is how others see you, which groups you belong to, and how others may describe you.

As a young child, most of your self-identity comes from your place in your family. But as you grow older, you start to identify more with your friends and peers. Some tweens may experience an '**identity crisis**' – a struggle they experience as their identity pulls in two different directions – towards childhood and towards adulthood.

During the pre-teen and teen years, young people may experience many different thoughts and feelings, such as:

- worrying about appearance, especially skin and hair
- feeling worried or anxious
- wishing for more independence from the family
- feeling embarrassed by family members
- feeling awkward or self-conscious about physical changes to body shape, appearance and voice

- experiencing bullying from peers
- social and emotional conflicts
- some old friendships may end and new ones may begin
- comparing oneself to one's peers
- trying out different roles – different ways of dressing, talking, different kinds of humour, and so on.

8

For questions 1 to 3, circle the correct answer. For questions 4 to 6, write or draw your answers.

1. The pre-adolescent years are the years between:
   a 13 to 19
   b 6 to 9
   c 9 to 12

2. Which of the following is NOT part of your social identity:
   a how you see yourself
   b your school grades
   c the groups you belong to

3. Which word does not match?
   a pre-teen
   b adolescent
   c tween

4. Explain the difference between self-identity and social identity.

   _____
   _____
   _____
   _____

5. Explain in your own words what you understand by the 'identity crisis' faced by some pre-adolescents.

   _____

6. Choose one of the struggles described on page 8. Work in pairs or groups. Develop a role play dramatising this struggle. Use your role play to draw a cartoon strip.

9

Unit 2 Our groups

Games and clubs

1. Team sports and games are fun for everyone, but they are especially **beneficial** for teens and pre-teens. Read what the students below say about their games and clubs, then answer the questions that follow.

HINT
'Beneficial' means providing benefits. Benefits are things that help us or offer us something useful.

> Running keeps my body strong and fit, and it always lifts my mood.

> It also helps me sleep well. Then I have more energy the next day too.

> We play basketball at the community centre. It's fun spending time with other kids our age.

> It's good exercise too, and you learn to work in a team and communicate with others.

> It's great being part of a team and working together.

> Yes, we have to think as a team, discuss and work together to develop a winning game plan.

> I always feel good about the world after some time singing in our choir.

> It also feels good to develop a talent and a skill, and to feel like you belong to a group of people that share your interest.

a List eight different benefits that the students in the pictures have noticed from their participation in sports and other activities.

_____
_____
_____
_____
_____
_____
_____

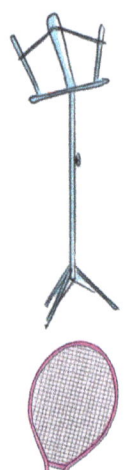

b Why do you think team sports and games are especially helpful for teens and pre-teens? Write your ideas here.

_____
_____
_____

2 Which team sports or games do you participate in? Are you a member of a club? Find out more about clubs in your school or community.

_____

_____

3 How does your community make an effort to provide team games for young people? Write the activities that are available in your community.

Activities at school	Activities at local community centres

Church activities	Other activities

Revise and prepare

1. Jessie lives with her grandparents, aunt, parents and siblings. Which word best describes her family type? (1)

    a sibling   b nuclear   c extended

2. Draw a picture of a nuclear family. (2)

3. Describe one advantage and one disadvantage of living in each type of family:

    a nuclear family (2)

    _____
    _____

    b extended family (2)

    _____
    _____

4. Identify which of the following can cause conflict among family members: (1)

    a speaking respectfully to others and listening patiently
    b shouting to make yourself heard
    c helping others with their chores.

5. A role model is: (1)

    a an older sibling
    b someone who can drive
    c someone that others can look up to as an example.

12

6 Choose two of the qualities presented below. Define each quality chosen and give an example which demonstrates each quality through mature behaviour. (4)

humility   kindness   service   care   responsibility

_____
_____
_____
_____
_____

7 Identify which one is NOT a reason that a pre-adolescent may experience an 'identity crisis':
    a   their identity is changing from that of child to that of adult
    b   there may be changes in their social groups
    c   there is something wrong with them. (1)

8 List eight ways that team games benefit young adolescents. (8)

_____
_____
_____
_____
_____
_____
_____
_____

9 Identify a club at your school, and explain how it benefits the students that take part. (3)

_____
_____
_____
_____
_____

(TOTAL: 25 marks)

 Locating my community

Using maps and plans

An **aerial** photograph is a picture taken looking directly down on an area of land. It helps us to see exactly where everything is. How is an aerial photograph taken?

This aerial photograph (right) and plan map (below) show the same place.

Key
- 🎾 sports centres
- ✝ place of worship
- 🎓 place of study
- Ⓗ place of historical importance
- 📖 library
- Ⓣ transport
- 🏪 store
- 🍴 restaurant

1. What is the same about the two pictures? What is different?

2. Find each place on the plan map first, and mark it with the correct letter. Then find it on the aerial photograph and mark it with the correct letter there.

   A   the basketball courts

   B   the university library

   C   the Campus War Memorial

   D   St. David's Hall

   E   the bus route

3. Use the 8-point compass to help you determine the directions north, south, east, west.

4. Using the plan map for clues, work out in which direction you would need to walk to get:

   a   from the research institute to the university bookshop

   b   from the bookshop to the library

   c   from the basketball courts to St. David's Hall.

5. a   Use an atlas to help you work out which island this map is from.

   b   What is the name of the bay to the south of the university?

   c   Name two neighbouring communities near to this university.

   d   Name the nearest Caribbean country to the north and to the south of this island.

   e   Before we had satellite technology, how do you think people made aerial photographs?

Land use

Land and water are important resources that we use in many different ways. A land use map shows how people use the land in different ways. It may use colours, symbols or different kinds of shading to indicate how each area is used. Here is a land use map of St. Lucia.

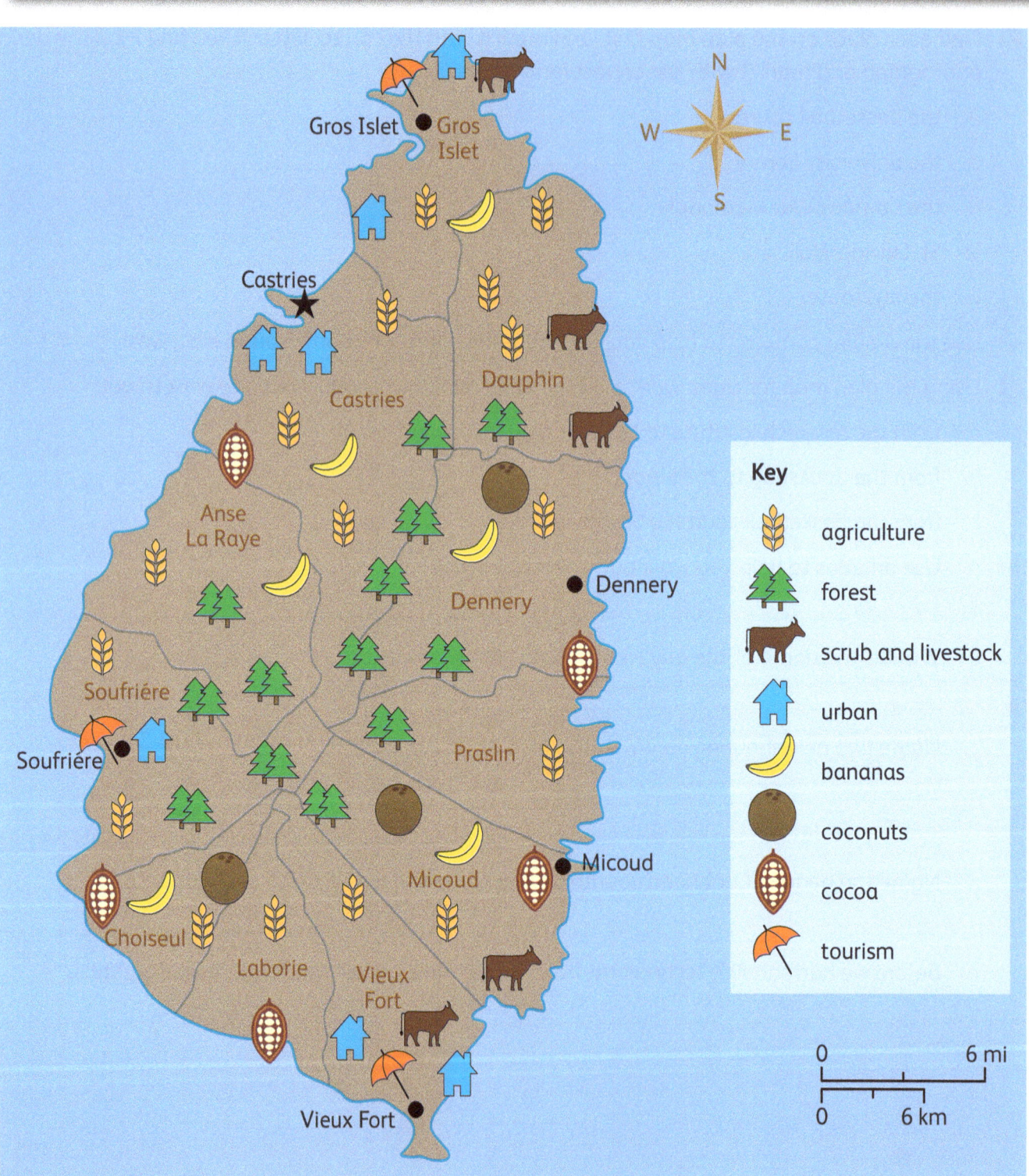

For questions 1 to 3, circle the correct answer. Then answer the rest of the questions.

1 Look at the land usage on the coastline as compared to land usage in the interior.

Most of the land in St. Lucia is:

a used for houses and buildings

b used for farming

c covered in forest.

2 Most of St. Lucia's population live:

a along the coast

b in the north

c in the forest

3 The forested area is mostly:

a in the centre

b in the south-west

c in the south-east

4 Why do you think there are fewer 🏠 symbols in the centre of the island?

_____

5 Use an electronic map or an atlas. Locate your own community.

a Tick (✔) the types of land use that take place in your community:

　🌲　forest　☐

　🌾　agriculture　☐

　🐄　livestock　☐

　🏠　urban (housing)　☐

　⛱　tourism　☐

b Name one or more neighbouring communities that are near to your area on a map.

_____

c Identify the features that mark the boundaries between your community and a neighbouring community. Tick (✔) any that apply, or describe the boundary markers.

☐ mountain　☐ river　☐ fence　☐ sign　☐ road　☐ other

_____
_____
_____

4 Heritage

Important events in our history

The Caribbean is made up of many nations, and we share a similar history with some local differences. The culture, festivals and celebrations in each territory also show similarities and differences.

Read the history of the Tainos or Amerindian people in your textbook.

What are the names of the other early people who inhabited the Caribbean territories? How were they different from each other? How were they similar to each other?

Stories of bravery and determination

The mid-1500s to the 1860s were a horrific period for African people. During this time, approximately 12.5 million African people were enslaved and brought to the Americas to work on plantations. About 4 million of these people were delivered to the Caribbean, to work mostly in gold and silver mines, or on plantations growing sugar, coffee, tobacco or cotton.

Nanny of the maroons

- Life on the plantations was brutal and harsh, and it was nearly impossible to escape.
- However, some enslaved Africans, known as **maroons**, escaped to form their own communities.
- The maroon communities had their own culture, government and trade.
- Some maroon communities managed to establish treaties with the colonial rulers. Examples include groups in Jamaica and St. Vincent and the Grenadines and the maroons in Suriname.
- In the early 1700s, a woman called Nanny escaped from slavery.
- She formed a community called Nanny Town in the Blue Mountain region of Jamaica.
- She trained maroon warriors who fought against the British for many years.
- Nanny is a national heroine in Jamaica.

1. What other stories have you heard about Nanny? Do your own research and write what you find out.

Unit 4 Heritage

Toussaint Louverture

- In 1743, Toussaint Louverture was born in Saint-Domingue, a French colony on the island of Hispaniola.

- He was one of the enslaved Africans who worked on the sugar cane and coffee plantations.

- Although he was born a slave, he enjoyed reading and became well-educated.

- When he was 33 years old he was freed. He began to build up his own property and wealth. He was a **revolutionary** who thought that enslaved people should fight for their freedom and **autonomy**.

- He was a leader of the Haitian Revolution. His leadership and bravery showed millions of free and enslaved Africans around the world that it was possible to **overthrow** their **colonial** rulers and achieve **liberation**.

- In 1789, the French Revolution took place in France, where the poor and peasants rose up to demand the right to vote.

- In 1791, inspired by the French Revolution, the enslaved people of Saint-Domingue began their own rebellion against the white plantation owners, with Toussaint Louverture as their leader.

- He took his name L'ouverture from the French word for 'opening', because he was so skilled at finding openings in enemy lines. The Haitian Revolution lasted 12 years.

- In 1801, Toussaint declared a Constitution for a free, autonomous republic, stating that he would be its leader for life. The Constitution stated that slavery would be abolished under French law.

- Toussaint was arrested by the French and died in prison, and slavery was briefly reinstated by Napoleon.

- However, by 1804, Haiti became a new independent republic.

1. From the text, work out or look up definitions for the words in bold.

key words

overthrow ....

....

colonial ....

....

liberation ....

....

revolutionary ....

....

autonomy ....

....

2. Which important event in Europe led to the enslaved African uprisings in the colonies?

3. Which 12-year event led to the establishment of a free republic in Haiti, without enslaved Africans?

4. Look at the portrait of Toussaint Louverture. What does the picture try to show about him? Explain how the artist gives us information about him.

Unit 4 Heritage

Marcus Garvey

- In 1887, Marcus Garvey was born in Jamaica.
- At 14, Marcus left school to work as a printer's **apprentice**. While he worked at the printing press, he led a strike for higher wages for workers there.
- Between 1910 and 1912, Marcus went travelling. He saw South and Central America, and also visited Britain.
- In 1914 he returned to Jamaica and founded the Universal Negro Improvement Association (UNIA).
- In 1916 he moved to New York, where UNIA became a growing **movement**. His movement and ideas gained great popularity and became known as 'Garveyism'.
- His message to **African-Americans** was that they should be proud to be black.
- He spoke about Africa's history before the arrival of colonial settlers.
- He believed that black people should 'unite, **emancipate** and improve'.
- Although he wished to return to Jamaica, he stayed in America in order to help the **civil rights movement**.
- He believed that black people needed to establish their own businesses in order to develop economic strength.
- In 1964, 26 years after his death, Marcus Garvey was declared Jamaica's first national hero.

1 Use a dictionary to help you understand the words in bold. Write your own definitions here.

key words

apprentice ....
movement ....
African-American ....
emancipate ....
civil rights movement ....

2 Identify two ways that Marcus Garvey worked selflessly to help others.

3 Why do you think the US government did not like Garveyism?

4 Why is Marcus Garvey considered a Jamaican national hero?

Creating and displaying works of art

1. Choose one of your national heroes and heroines. You will create a work of art about them together with your class.

2. Choose your media – the materials you will use for your artwork. These might include any of the following: paint, pencils, crayons, chalk, paper, fabrics, glue, found objects or any other media.

3. Sketch a rough design for your artwork below. Then create a square artwork. Finally, work with your class to arrange all the squares together to create a composite artwork called 'Heritage'. Display it at your school.

Unit 4 Heritage

Traditional work roles

Gemma wanted to find out more about traditional work roles in the Caribbean. She asked her granny two questions:

- What kinds of work did people traditionally do in rural communities in the past?
- How have work roles been modernised?

I grew up on a **rural** farm, with my siblings and cousins. People had big families, and everyone helped and worked. We lived with my mother and my grandparents. The women and girls in the family, we had to look after the little ones, and do all the cooking and household chores. We kids had to leave school early to help with the work. We grew vegetables, and kept chickens and goats. My mother earned extra money selling her homemade goodies and cakes. My Auntie worked as a cleaner. She also wove baskets to sell at the market. The men in the village worked mostly in fishing and farming. Some worked in building and construction. Everyone in the community worked together to build homes and roads, or cultivate the garden.

Today, the farm that we lived on has been **modernised**. It has an **eco-lodge** and tourists come to visit. Some of my grandchildren have even been to college and they work as computer programmers, and managers at the lodge. Nobody had that kind of work when I was growing up.

1. 'Rural' means:
   a   in poor areas
   b   in the city rather than in the country
   c   in the country rather than in the city

2. Name six different kinds of work that the women carried out.

___

3. Name four kinds of work that the men carried out.

___

4. Are these work roles similar or different to the ones that you see adults doing today? What is similar? What is different?

___

Unit 4 Heritage

Modernisation

Modernisation is a process of changing traditional roles and practices to adapt to contemporary (present) society. We can see modernisation in many things – clothing, communication, building and design. Work roles have also changed in many ways.

Discuss how each picture on this page shows a way that traditional work roles are becoming modernised. Write your ideas under each picture.

Research

1. Speak to an older person and answer the following questions.

   a What kinds of work did people in your family do when you were growing up?
   _____
   _____
   _____

   b Which kinds of work in your community were well-paid, and which were not?
   _____
   _____

   c Did men and women have different work roles? If so, how did they differ?
   _____
   _____
   _____
   _____

   d What has changed the most in the work roles in your community?
   _____
   _____

2. If possible, take photographs of people working in traditional work roles that still exist today. You can glue or draw the pictures here.

5 Caribbean groupings

Cooperation and integration

When we talk about the Caribbean region, we might mean different things:

* countries in our area – the countries that are situated in and near the Caribbean Sea
* our geographical location – the landforms and oceans between the continents of North and South America
* political or cultural groups, such as the Organisation of Eastern Caribbean States (OECS) or the Caribbean Community (CARICOM).

The Caribbean is made up of many small countries. We may be different nations, but we have many things in common:

* ancestry – Amerindian, European, African, Indian and Chinese
* similar histories of pre-colonial culture, colonisation, slavery and independence
* geographic formations as island-states, with tropical vegetation and climates
* small country sizes and small populations
* shared risk of natural disasters as we live in the same geographic zone
* scarcity of resources in each country.

The Caribbean region is large, but each individual country is small. When we form groupings with other countries, we are able to share our expertise and resources. We are also able to assist each other to get all the goods and services we need.

❶ Define the word 'cooperate'.
_____

❷ Suggest two ways that people can cooperate to benefit each other:

a   at school
_____
_____

b   in a family
_____
_____

c   in a neighbourhood
_____
_____

CARIFTA

Do research to complete this fact file about CARIFTA.

fact file

- CARIFTA stands for ....
- Date it was founded: ....
- Countries that first signed: ....
- Name of the treaty they signed: ....
- Countries that joined later: ....
- Explain the aims of CARIFTA: ....
  ....
- Date CARIFTA ended: ....

Colour all the islands or countries that were members of CARIFTA in 1972. For islands that are too small, put a coloured dot next to their names.

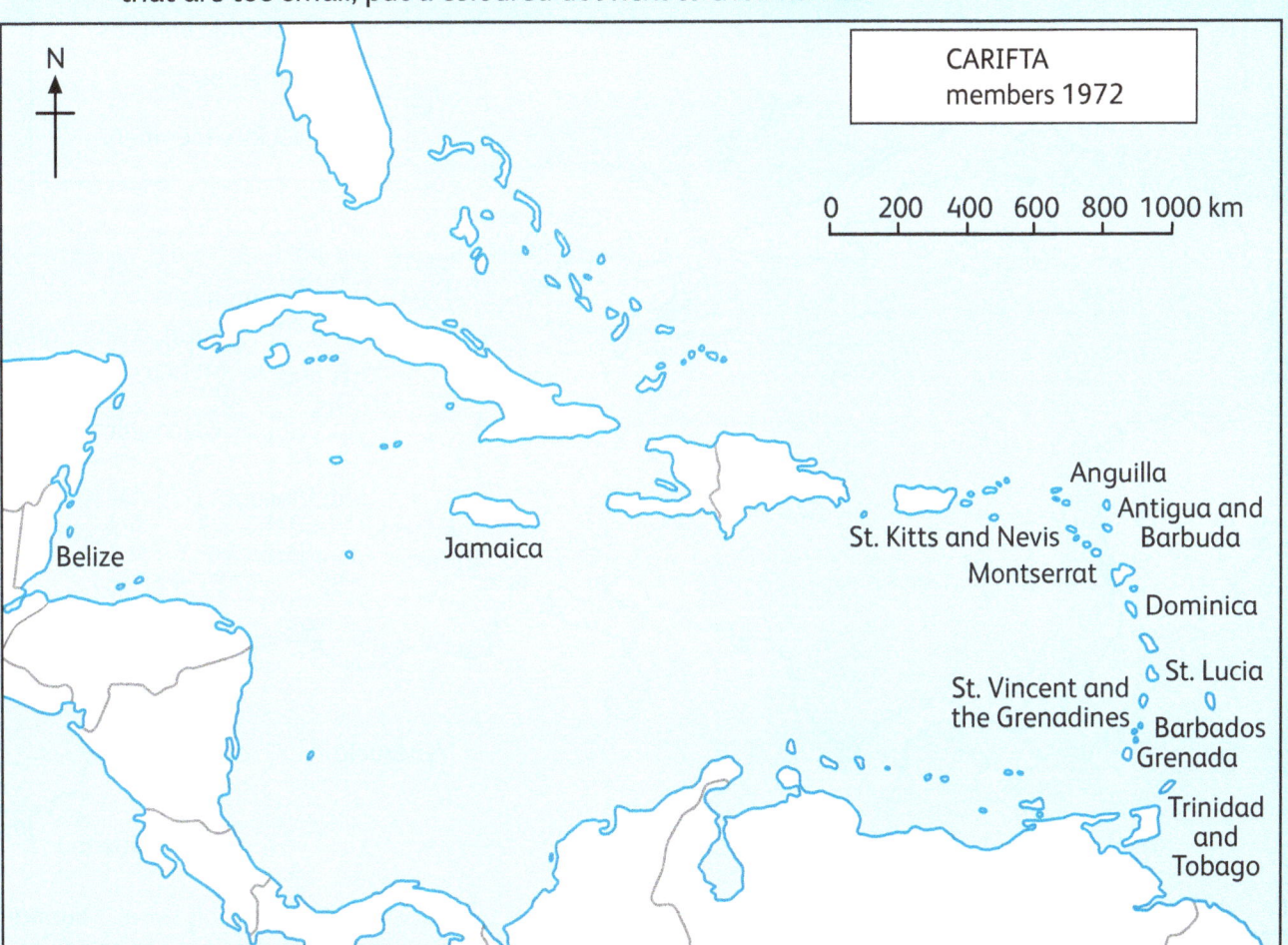

29

Unit 5 Caribbean groupings

CARICOM

Do your own research to complete this fact file about CARICOM.

fact file

- CARICOM stands for ....
- What is CARICOM? ....
- Date it was formed: ....
- Name of the treaty they signed: ....
- Location of headquarters: ....
- Original signatories and name of treaty: ....
....

Find out which countries are full members and which are associate members. Create a colour key and show this information on the map.

KEY
CARICOM countries
☐ Full members
☐ Associate members

Map of the Caribbean showing: Mexico, Belize, The Bahamas, Cayman Islands, Turks and Caicos, Haiti, Dominican Republic, Puerto Rico, British Virgin Islands, Anguilla, Antigua and Barbuda, Montserrat, Dominica, St. Kitts and Nevis, Jamaica, St. Vincent and the Grenadines, St. Lucia, Barbados, Grenada, Aruba, Netherlands Antillies, Trinidad and Tobago, Venezuela, Colombia, Guyana, Suriname, Atlantic Ocean, Caribbean Sea. Scale: 0 200 400 600 800 1000 km.

CARICOM's work and sub-groups

The original aims of CARICOM were:

- to encourage trade between members
- to allow the region to stand together when dealing with outside countries
- to encourage cooperation in education, sports, health, technology and transport.

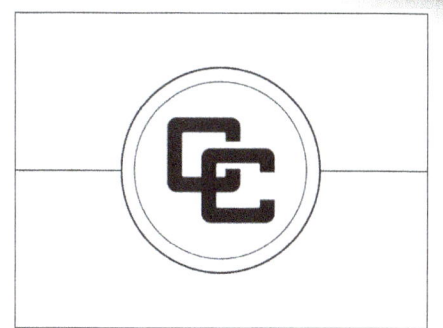

Over the years CARICOM has added many more aims. Do research to find out as many of these as you can.

① Colour the CARICOM flag. Find out what each symbol represents.

The 2 Cs represent _____

The light blue at the top represents _____

The dark blue at the bottom represents _____

The yellow circle represents _____

The ring of green represents _____

Because CARICOM has so many aims, it has many institutions that deal with specific areas of work.

② Work in pairs or small groups to research one organisation from this list: CDEMA, CTU, CXC, CMI, CMO, CFC, CFNI, CARCAE, CEHI, CARDI. Only acronyms are given here. Full names are on pages 112 and 135 of your textbook. For each organisation, find out the date it was founded and three things it does. Report on your findings to your class. Take notes as other groups report.

Unit 5 Caribbean groupings

Benefits of cooperation

1. Write your own ideas about the benefits of cooperation between Caribbean countries. You can write examples from your own life and family, or think of ways that people all over the Caribbean benefit from cooperation in these areas.

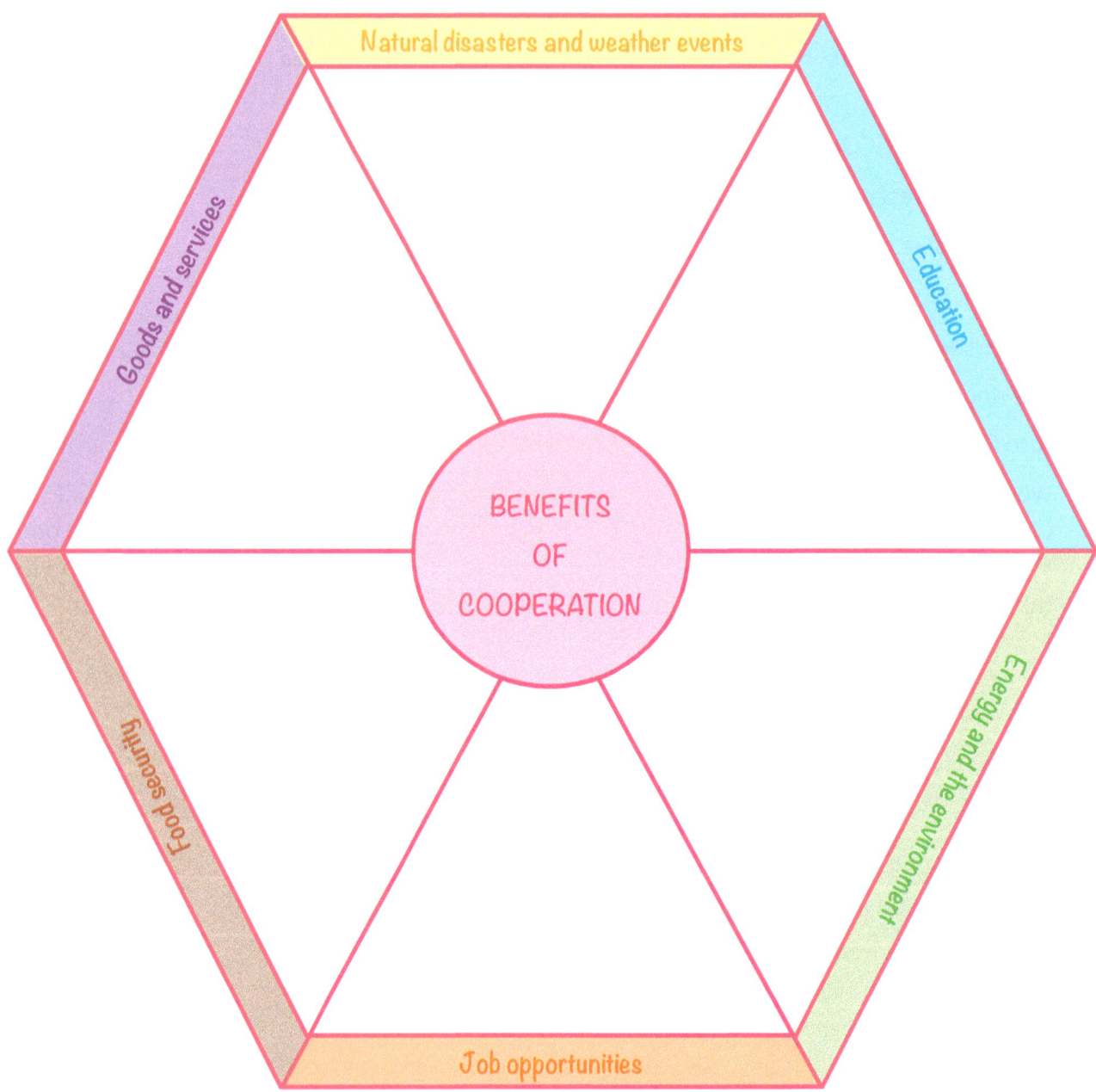

2. Look up and define:

key words

integration ....

interdependence ....

Revise and prepare

① Identify which of the following might be shown on a land use map: (1)

   a tourist attractions, cafés and shops   b climate regions and vegetation

   c industrial zones, farm areas, bodies of water, vacant land

② Identify which of the following is NOT a boundary between communities: (1)

   a a river that marks the division between two parishes   b a church spire in a town square

   c a dotted line on a map showing a country border

③ Use the map below to help you answer the questions.

   a The airport in the north of Dominica is called _____ and the one in the southeast is _____. (2)

   b NP stands for National Park. Name the national park just to the west of the Melville Hall River. _____ (1)

   c The southernmost town is called _____. (1)

   d If you are going from Pont Casse to Castle Bruce, which natural feature would you visit along the way? _____ (1)

4 Choose one of the people you have learnt about who exhibited selflessness, bravery or determination. Briefly write who they were, when they lived, and what they did to contribute to our Caribbean heritage. (3)

5 Agnes grows her own vegetables at home. This way of providing food for the family is best described as: (1)

    a   traditional   b   external   c   modern

6 In a modernised society, people are likely to communicate by: (1)

    a   notices in the daily newspaper

    b   email and instant messaging

    c   notes on a community noticeboard.

7 Identify which of the following are traditional forms of work: (1)

    a   call-centre assistant, computer programmer and software designer

    b   hotel manager, PR consultant and social media advisor

    c   fisherman, cleaner, stonemason, carpenter

8 List any four aims of CARICOM. (4)

9 Explain three benefits of cooperation and integration in the Caribbean region. (3)

(TOTAL: 20 marks)

6 National identity

Identifying ourselves

Have you ever waved hello to a friend, only to realise as the person came closer that you had mistaken them for someone else? Usually, we recognise people we know in a variety of **informal** ways – their face, their way of dressing, their accent and their voice. Partially sighted or blind people even rely on recognising others by touch and by smell. However, sometimes we need to identify ourselves to people who do not know us personally. For example, when you open a bank account, or sign for a parcel at the post office, or cross the border into a new country, you are expected to show a **form of identification** or **ID**.

1. Describe three ways that you recognise your friends when you see them from a distance away.

2. In each situation below, the person has to show a form of ID. Match the best form of ID to each situation.

   a. Miles is picking up a disability grant that he receives each month.

   b. Julia gets stopped on her motorbike by a traffic officer.

   c. Caroline's parents want to enrol her at a new school.

   d. Dennis works at a bank. He has to use a special ID to be allowed access to some areas at work.

   e. Alisa is taking a plane from Barbados to Jamaica.

3. List three other situations where you might need to show a form of identification.

4. Members of CARICOM share a similar passport. Compare and contrast the passports of different islands.

Unit 6 National identity

Applying for documents

When you apply for official documents, you fill in forms. Your **signature** shows you agree to the document you have signed. It should be similar each time you do it. You may need to provide **biometrics** – biological data such as **fingerprints** and eye scans.

Even though it is possible that two people may have similar fingerprints, the chances are so tiny that a fingerprint is a very good form of biometric identification.

① Do you have a signature that you have practised? Practise your signature here. Try it at least four times. Circle the one you like the best.

② Practise filling in the form below. Use capital letters and black ink. Use some ink or watery paint to make a fingerprint.

SURNAME
NAME
DATE OF BIRTH D D M M Y Y Y Y
PLACE OF BIRTH
NAME OF PARENT OR GUARDIAN
ADDRESS

CONTACT NUMBER
ALTERNATE CONTACT NUMBER
IDENTIFICATION NUMBER
SIGNATURE   DATE

LEFT THUMBPRINT   RIGHT THUMBPRINT

③ Why do you think it is important to use signatures and fingerprints in identification?

36

My national identity

In any country, there are certain events that bring people together, creating a sense of **unity** in the nation. A government may create social and cultural programmes that help unify the nation. Examples are sports programmes, arts programmes, festivals and cultural days.

❶ Write a paragraph about a sporting or cultural programme that unifies your country. Include details about what it is, when it takes place, and why people enjoy it.

_____
_____
_____
_____

My country is _____. My nationality is _____.

❷ Imagine that you are travelling abroad. Sitting in a train, you notice a family that comes from the same country as you. Suggest how you might notice this based on:

a appearance

_____
_____

b language

_____
_____

c accent

_____
_____

d a recognisable event that they might be discussing

_____
_____
_____

❸ What makes you most proud of your country?

_____
_____

Unit 6 National identity

Key people in my country

Each country has its own national heroes. Read about some of these national heroes from different countries in the Caribbean.

Mabel 'Cissie' Caudeiron

Cissie Caudeiron was a folklorist from Dominica. She inspired a revival of popular Dominican culture – music, songs, dances and folklore.

Chief Joseph Chatoyer

On March 14th, the people of St. Vincent and the Grenadines celebrate their national hero, the Carib Chief Joseph Chatoyer.

Papa Bird/Vere Cornwall Bird

Antigua National Heroes Day is celebrated on December 9th, the birthday of Sir Vere Cornwall Bird. He was the first prime minister of Antigua and Barbuda, and known as Papa Bird, the father of the nation. Other heroes are King Court, who led a slave revolt in the 1700s, Dame Georgiana Ellen (Nellie) Robinson, who improved the education system, and Sir Vivian Richards, one of the greatest cricket players from the West Indies.

1. Does your country celebrate National Heroes Day? If so, on which date?

2. Who are your country's national heroes?

3. Choose one hero to research. Write three sentences about them here.

7 Travel and migration

Customs officers

Read about the work of a customs officer and answer the questions.

> I am a customs officer. My job involves a lot of responsibility. I help to enforce the laws of the country, by checking the identity and travel history of each person who arrives at the border. Customs officers work at all the border entry points: seaports and airports. In other countries, they also work at road border posts.
>
> We also check goods and baggage that come into the country. We question some people in order to find out if they are any risk to the country. If they have prior offences, we may question them about that.
>
> We search baggage for smuggled items such as drugs, weapons and illegal imports. We also help in the fight against the illegal trade in endangered species of birds and animals. If people are bringing goods legally into the country, they may need to declare those goods and pay duties on them. We collect data about the goods coming in, and deal with revenue on these imports.

1. Who is a customs officer?

2. Why do we need customs officers at all ports of entry?

3. Why is a customs officer's job important to the country? Explain what could happen if we did not have customs officers.

4. Suggest three questions that a customs officer may ask someone who is arriving at a port.

Unit 7 Travel and migration

Boat and ship services

Because the Caribbean has many island nations separated by sea, an important route of transport in our region is the sea. This makes boat and ship services very important for passengers as well as cargo.

❶ Choose another country in the OECS or CARICOM that you wish to visit. Find out two different passenger boat services you could use to get there. Write about each one:

- Name of the service
- Length and cost of the journey
- What is included in the service.

Explain which one you would choose and why.

❷ Imagine that your family is moving to the island you chose to visit. You need to send a container of household goods to that island. Identify two different cargo boat services that you could send your goods with. Identify the name of the service and find out what they charge to send a container of goods, as well as the time it would take to ship.

❸ On this map of the Caribbean, draw some routes of the shipping services you researched.

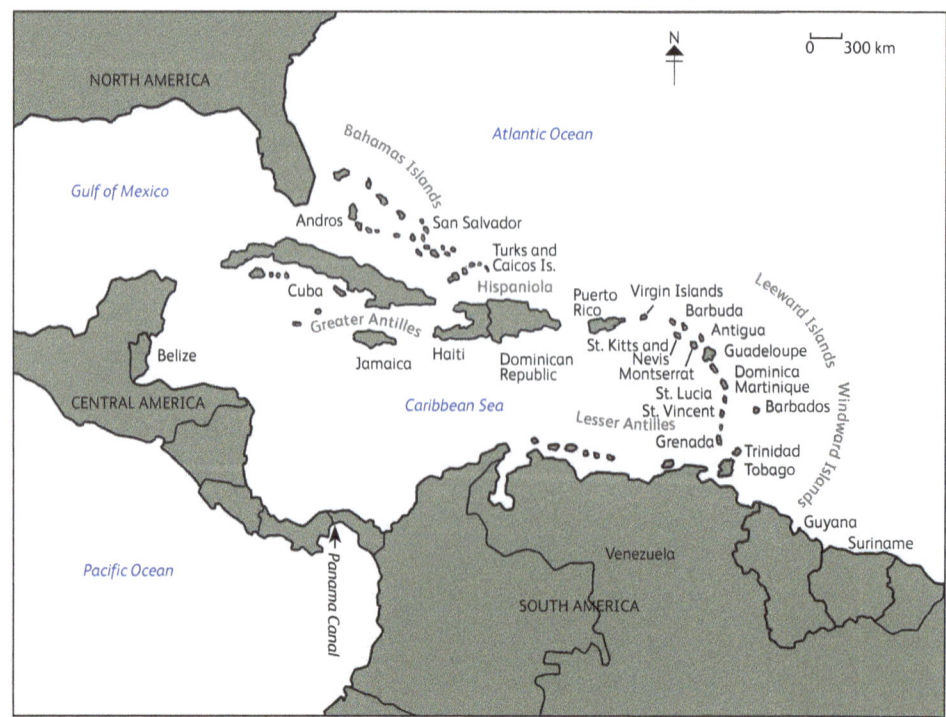

Airline routes

1 Another way that we can travel in the Caribbean is by plane. Find out the names of some of the airlines that connect the islands in the Caribbean.

Names of airlines:

_____
_____
_____
_____
_____
_____

2 Name eight other islands in the region. Find out which airline flies to each island, and the duration of the flight from your country to each of these.

_____
_____
_____
_____
_____
_____
_____
_____
_____
_____

3 Why is it important that we have airlines and shipping lines that connect OECS and CARICOM countries and the wider world? What would happen if we could not travel within and beyond our region? Write a paragraph with your ideas.

8 Human rights

The Universal Declaration of Human Rights

All human beings are entitled to **human rights** and these rights are protected by laws. For example, everyone has the right to live freely without fear of violence. The **Universal Declaration of Human Rights** (UDHR) is a statement that was adopted in 1948 at a General Assembly of the United Nations (UN).

1. Find the full text of the UDHR at *https://www.un.org/en/universal-declaration-human-rights/*. Use the Declaration to help you to decide whether each statement is true or false. After each statement is a clue about which Article to read. If it is false, correct the statement.

   a. You have the right to freedom from prejudice, bias or stereotyping based on your race, gender, nationality or religion. (Article 2)

   b. Some people have the right to be free from slavery. (Article 4)

   c. Your government may arrest or imprison you for any reason. (Article 9)

   d. Consenting adults have the right to marry and raise a family. (Article 16)

   e. Parents may decide not to educate their children if they do not wish to. (Article 26)

   f. No country, group or person may use this declaration to deny the rights or freedoms of others. (Article 30)

2. Choose any other Article from the Declaration. Explain what it says and why you believe it is important.

Rights and freedoms in our Constitution

Each country has its own particular way of stating the rights and freedoms of its citizens. You can find these in your country's **Constitution**. A Constitution is a **legal document**, and it may be very long, with very **formal language**. The statements are known as **provisions** or **clauses**, and they are usually numbered, sometimes with letters for each sub-clause. Here are some tips for finding the rights and freedoms within your Constitution.

* Find the Contents section. Is there a particular section or chapter that deals with rights and freedoms? Look for these key words: **fundamental human rights**, **rights enshrined**, **freedoms**

* Go to the section that deals with these rights. Some Constitutions will have notes alongside the main text indicating the topic of each article or provision. Use these to help you.

Research your country's Constitution. Your school may have a printed copy, or you may be able to find it on the internet.

1. What is the title and date of your country's Constitution?
___

2. Quote the provision or clause from the Constitution that shows how your country protects each of the following basic human rights. Add a note of any responsibilities which are tied to each right (for example, freedom of speech includes the responsibility not to say things which discriminate against others or are illegal):

   a freedom to act according to one's own conscience
   ___

   b freedom to meet and gather peacefully in groups (freedom of assembly)
   ___

   c freedom of movement and travel: what responsibilities are tied to this right?
   ___

   d freedom of speech: what responsibilities are tied to this right?
   ___

Unit 8 Human rights

Human rights violations

> **Human rights violations** are situations where people are denied their rights or freedoms. They are also called **human rights abuses**. Even though most countries agree in principle to the universal rights of their citizens, violations do still take place.

❶ Read each speech bubble. Identify which human rights are being violated in each situation.

> I come from a very poor country. My family home does not have electricity or running water, because the government says they do not have enough money to provide for everyone.

> In my country, the government is very corrupt. My father was part of an opposition party and was speaking out against the government. One night, some police arrived in an unmarked vehicle and arrested him. We are worried for his safety.

> I work in a factory. The hours are very long, and the pay is very low. In order to earn enough for my family, I need to work as many hours as I can. I hardly get any time to rest. I worry that if I get ill, nobody will provide for us.

_____
_____
_____

❷ Think about the history you have learnt about your country. Write about at least two ways that human rights were violated in your country's history.

_____
_____
_____
_____
_____
_____

❸ In a newspaper or news website, read about current events in your country. Identify any situations where human rights are being violated.

_____
_____
_____
_____

44

The rights of children

Children have some special rights. The **Convention on the Rights of the Child** is an international declaration of these rights.

* All children have the right to a name, enough food to eat and a place to live.
* All children should be looked after when they are sick.
* Children have a right to grow up with love, affection and security.
* Disabled children have a right to special treatment and education.
* All children have a right to free education, and should be protected from neglect, cruelty and exploitation.
* Nobody is allowed to make children work before a certain age.
* Children must be protected from discrimination.

1 Read this extract from the Convention on the Rights of the Child:

Article 28

1. …
   (a) Make primary education compulsory and available free to all;
   (b) Encourage the development of different forms of secondary education, including general and vocational education, make them available and accessible to every child, and take appropriate measures such as the introduction of free education and offering financial assistance in case of need;
   (c) Make higher education accessible to all on the basis of capacity by every appropriate means;
   (d) Make educational and vocational information and guidance available and accessible to all children;
   (e) Take measures to encourage regular attendance at schools and the reduction of drop-out rates.
2. States Parties shall take all appropriate measures to ensure that school discipline is administered in a manner consistent with the child's human dignity and in conformity with the present Convention.

2 Summarise Article 28 in simple language so that the meaning is easier to understand.

Unit 8 Human rights

The right to education

Every child has the right to education. This creates many responsibilities for the government, for parents and for children themselves.

1 Brainstorm: what do parents, governments and children have to do to make sure that children get the education to which they are entitled?

Responsibilities

Parents	Government	Children

2 Find your country's Education Act either online or in a reference book.

   a Which part of the Act talks about parents' rights and responsibilities in their children's education?

   b Read this section and list three rights that parents have with respect to their child's education.

3 Explain why each statement is incorrect. Refer to your Education Act.

   a Parents have a responsibility to build schools and train teachers.

   b The government has to provide a teacher for each family.

   c All children must learn exactly the same things.

   d Teachers should never speak to parents about their children's behaviour or progress.

   e Under no circumstances may a child be educated at home.

   f Students have the right to freedom of speech and movement. This means that they can do whatever they like at school.

9 The justice system

What is justice?

Revenge
James broke Eric's Rubik's cube.
So Eric tore up James' schoolbooks.

Justice
Simone broke her neighbour's window. She apologised. The neighbour accepted the apology but asked that Simone get the window fixed.

1. What difference do the stories show between justice and revenge?

    Justice _____

    Revenge _____

2. How would Eric and James' story end if Eric sought justice rather than revenge? Rewrite it with a new ending.

    _____
    _____

3. How would Simone's story end if the neighbour sought revenge rather than justice?

    _____
    _____

4. Write your own definitions for:

    ### key words

    justice _____

    revenge _____

Unit 9 The justice system

The judicial system

The **judicial system** is also known as the **judiciary**. These are the courts, **magistrates** and **judges** that interpret and apply the law when people get into **disputes**, or break the law. The nature and seriousness of each case determines which court will hear the matter. A judiciary system is usually organised in **tiers**. If a matter cannot be resolved at the lowest tier, it may be moved to a higher court or authority.

Each country has its own system of lower-tier courts, sometimes known as **magistrates' courts**, that resolve cases within each parish or within the country. These cases may then be referred to the **Eastern Caribbean Supreme Court**. This region-wide court is made up of two parts: first, a case would go to the **High Court of Justice**, which hears cases from subordinate courts throughout the region. At the highest level is the **Eastern Caribbean Court of Appeal**.

In the wider Caribbean, the Caribbean Court of Justice (CCJ) settles issues among CARICOM countries, while some countries still recognise the Judicial Committee of the Privy Council (JCPC) in the United Kingdom as their highest Court of Appeal.

Find out more about your country's own structure of courts. Draw a tree diagram showing the different levels of courts in your country.

Matters examined by the court

Which matters are examined by each type of court? If possible, speak to an advocate, attorney-at-law, legal student or anyone working in the legal field. Find out examples of the kinds of matters that are heard in each type of court.

In the empty blocks, fill in some of the other types of court found within your country's judicial system. Some examples may include the Gun Court, Family Court, Drug Court or Industrial Court, depending on the country you are in.

Type of court	Example of the types of matters heard here
Eastern Caribbean Court of Appeal	
Supreme Court (Criminal)	
Supreme Court (Civil)	
Magistrates' Court	

Unit 9 The justice system

A visit to the court

Arrange to visit a court in your country. If this is not possible, interview someone who works in or studies the justice system, or do research in the library or on the internet. Find out more about each of the following careers.

Chief Justice

_____
_____
_____
_____
_____
_____

Judge

_____
_____
_____
_____
_____
_____

Magistrate

_____
_____
_____
_____
_____
_____

Prosecutor

_____
_____
_____
_____
_____
_____

Attorney or lawyer

_____
_____
_____
_____
_____
_____

Paralegal

_____
_____
_____
_____
_____
_____

Revise and prepare

1. Some of the following are universal human rights, and some are special rights of children. Mark the universal human rights H and the special rights of children C. Some answers may get both letters. (8)

   a   the right to be free from slavery

   b   the right to marry and raise a family

   c   the right to be registered with a name at birth

   d   the right to be presumed innocent until proven guilty in the eyes of the law

   e   the right to be cared for by their own parents if possible

   f   the right to freedom from prejudice or discrimination on the basis of race, gender, religion or beliefs

   g   the right to an education

   h   the right to move and travel freely

2. The document that a country provides to protect the rights of its citizens is usually known as: (1)

   a   a convention   b   a declaration   c   a Constitution

3. Human rights violations are also known as: (1)

   a   human rights abuses   b   human rights advice   c   enshrined human rights

4. Which of the following is not a violation of human rights? (1)

   a   Imprisoning someone without a trial

   b   Imprisoning someone for organising a gathering

   c   Imprisoning someone for a crime after a judge and jury find them guilty.

5. If a matter cannot be resolved within a parish court or high court within one of the countries in our region, it may be referred to the: (1)

   a   Magistrates' Court   b   Justice Court   c   Supreme Court

6. Draw a tree diagram or flow diagram showing the three main levels of courts in an OECS country. (3)

(TOTAL: 15 marks)

10 You can depend on me

Punctuality

When you start working, **punctuality** becomes very important. Punctuality means being on time for meetings and appointments. Some workplaces have **fixed office hours**. Some people work on **flexitime** – they can choose when to work, as long as they complete all the tasks they need to get done.

I start work at 4 p.m. The kitchen closes at 10.30 p.m., and the restaurant closes at 11.30 p.m.

I usually work at the office from 9 a.m. to 4.30 p.m. But some days I have client meetings later in the afternoon or evening too.

I get to school at 7.30 a.m., and leave at 3.30 p.m. Even if I don't have classes to teach, I have lessons to prepare, and staff meetings during the day.

① Why is it important to be punctual for meetings and appointments when you are working? Read the reasons given, and add more of your own.

- To have enough time to get through everything on the agenda
- To show respect to others that are attending
- To show professionalism
- To ensure that others can rely on you
- To demonstrate reliability

② Imagine that you are interviewing someone for a job. They arrive late for the interview. Describe the impression this creates.

52

Punctuality at school

Norms are things that people expect from us in wider society. Some examples of norms are: dressing appropriately for an occasion, using appropriate language and paying attention when listening to those who are older or more experienced than us. School helps us to practise and develop punctuality. For this reason, it is always important to:

* arrive at school on time
* hand in your school work on time, on or before the due date and at the correct time
* return to lessons punctually after breaktimes
* attend meetings with punctuality.

① Why do you think it is important for students to be punctual and regular in their school attendance? Suggest some of the consequences that may result from missing lessons.

② What are some of the positive outcomes that may come from being regular in your school attendance, and handing in your work on time?

③ Why do you think it is important for schools to develop the norm of punctuality?

④ Brainstorm ways to improve students' attendance at your own school. Jot down your ideas here.

⑤ Are there any other student behaviours you would like to improve at your school or in your community? Write about them here. Think creatively. Write your ideas about how you could work with others in your school or community to improve these behaviours.

11 Caring for each other

Special care

When you **care** for someone, you think about and provide for their needs. You may do things to protect them and help them. We usually care most about the people closest to us. However, some people in a community have a special need for care as they are unable to care for themselves.

Children, senior citizens and disabled people all require care.

1. What does it mean to you to take care of someone?

2. Give an example of someone in your life who has cared for you. Describe some things they did in order to take care of you.

3. Give an example of someone you have taken care of. Describe what kinds of things you did to care for this person.

4. Why do we need to care for elderly people (senior citizens)?

Caring for children

Parents care for their children in different ways. They provide **physical care** in the form of a home, food, clothing, medical care and all the things the child needs. They also provide **emotional care** – love, affection, and stability. Parents teach their many norms, such as politeness, healthy habits, and personal hygiene. Parents may guide and correct their child's **behaviour** in order to teach them what is considered appropriate in their community.

1. For each situation, identify what the parent is doing to care for the child. Explain what would happen if the parent did not do this.

_____

_____

_____

_____

2. Write a paragraph describing what happens if parents do not pay attention to and care about their children's behaviour.

_____

_____

_____

_____

Unit 11 Caring for each other

When parents cannot take care of their children

Sometimes, parents are not able to care for their children. There are many circumstances that may cause this.

* **Poverty** may force a parent to leave their child in search of food or work.
* **Mental health issues**, **alcoholism** or **drug abuse** may mean parents are unable to care for their child.
* If there is violence or conflict in the home, children may suffer.
* Some children are **orphans**, whose parents have died – by illness, or accident or other causes.

It is never a child's fault that their parents are unable to take care of them. Every child has a right to care. Sometimes the state may step in to provide care, for example through an orphanage or foster home. Sometimes other families in the community are able to provide care.

1. Suggest three possible reasons that a parent may not be able to care for their own children.

2. On page 5 you learnt about different types of families. Explain how the extended family can provide a home for children who cannot stay with their parents.

3. Imagine that your family decides to foster a child who cannot stay with their own parent. Think of three ways that you could help the new arrival feel cared for in your family.

Revise and prepare

1. Choose the best definition of punctuality. (1)
   a. speaking respectfully to your elders
   b. being helpful and caring
   c. being on time for meetings, appointments and commitments.

2. George has a job interview. He decides to get his haircut half an hour before the interview and then rush there as fast as he can. What advice would you give him? (2)

3. Suggest two possible consequences of arriving late for a job interview. (2)

4. Schools help us develop punctuality by: (1)
   a. making us wear a uniform
   b. having fixed times for lessons, and deadlines for assignments
   c. arranging job shadow programmes.

5. Write your own definition of what it means to care for someone. (2)

6. Which two groups particularly need to be taken care of? (2)

7. Suggest two negative outcomes that may result when parents do not properly care about their children's behaviour. (2)

(TOTAL: 12 marks)

12 Telecommunication

Modern telecommunication

Communication is the sending and receiving of **messages** from one individual or group to another. Humans have communicated using gestures, words and written symbols for thousands of years. **Telecommunication** is the term we use to describe communication over a distance, for example by telephone or the internet. Some forms of telecommunication are sent from one sender to one receiver. Others are **broadcast** to millions of people at the same time.

1876	**1926**	**1946**	**1973**	**1992**	**2001 to present**
The first telephone used landline technology. The sound travelled along wires.	The first transatlantic call was placed from London to New York.	Area codes allowed people to call directly from one location to another.	The first mobile phone was a large brick-shaped device, the first telephone that did not require wires.	The first SMS (short message service) was sent from one mobile to another.	Increasing improvements in wireless technology and internet service (internet, WiFi, smartphones, apps, cloud computing and more).

1 Describe a form of modern communication that you would use to:

    a find out about weather conditions in another country _____

    b book a flight to another island _____

    c speak to a relative in the next village _____

    d listen to the news while in a car _____

    e listen to music while on a bus _____

2 In 1876, the telephone was the newest technology. Explain three ways that this technology was improved later in the 1900s.

3 Name three new technologies that were developed after 2001. For each one, say how it benefitted the way we could communicate.

Obstacles to communication

> **Obstacles** to communication are things that prevent us from communicating, or make communication slow or difficult. Communication obstacles may have **technological** or **human** causes. Technological causes include technology not working properly, working too slowly or channels breaking down. Human causes include lack of knowledge, skill or training, or decisions that make it harder for people to communicate.

I'd love to call my family more often, but they are often not at home.

I don't make a lot of calls because call charges are so expensive.

Mobile coverage in my area is unreliable as we don't have 4G or 5G towers.

Sometimes people cannot reach me as the battery life on my phone is very short.

My internet is very slow, and sometimes it does not work.

1 Which of the obstacles mentioned above are human obstacles, and which are technological? Note them in this table.

Human	Technological

2 Suggest ways that some of the human obstacles you noticed could be removed.

_____

_____

3 Think of ways to remove obstacles to communication. Add your own ideas below.

Removing communication obstacles

Human

Technological
- companies could lower call charges
- governments could budget for free internet in some areas
- training programmes for setting up websites
- more ICT training in schools

Unit 12 Telecommunication

Benefits of technology

Technology has become an important part of the way we design cars, planes and other modes of transport. You have probably seen some of the following communication systems:

Fuel light

Oil light

Door open alert

Fasten seatbelt alert

① Explain to a partner how each of these alerts can make a car safer.

_____
_____
_____
_____

② What other communication systems have you seen or heard in a car? Explain what they look or sound like, and how they make the car safer.

_____
_____
_____
_____

③ Read about some of the newer features that modern cars use to make them safer.

Park assist technology uses cameras and radars to allow a car to park in a tight space without bumping into anything.

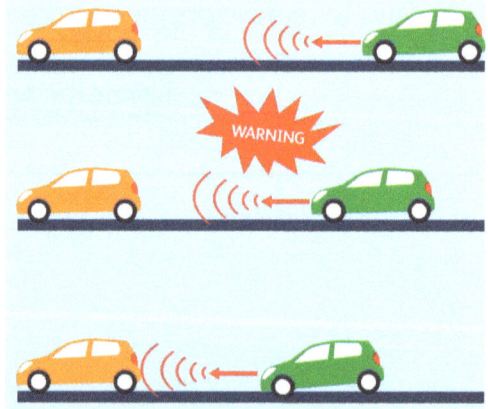

Automatic braking systems (ABS) use sensors to automatically deploy brakes, preventing collisions.

Lane detection systems show the driver how well they are keeping centred in their own lane.

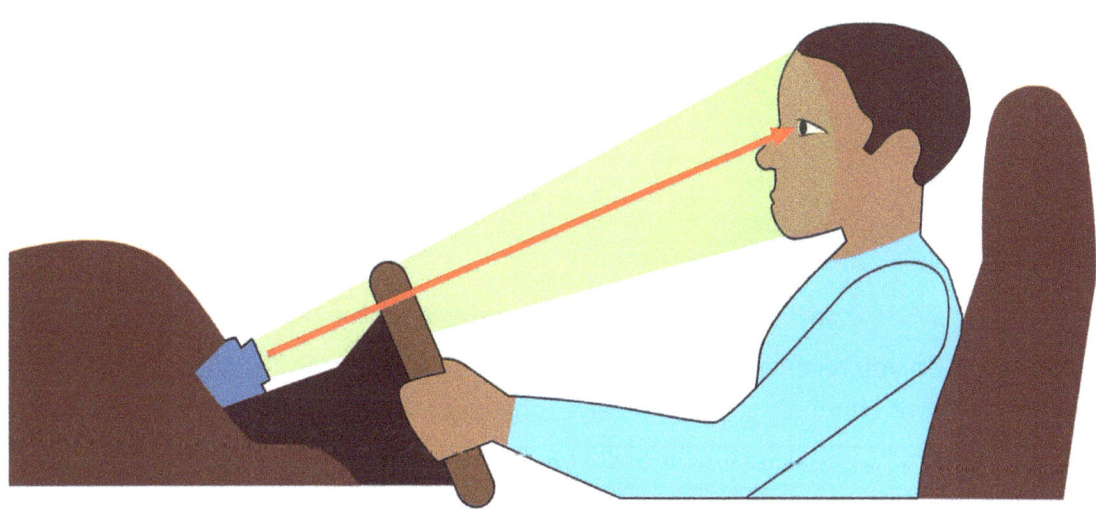

Driver alertness monitoring uses facial recognition technology. If the sensors detect that the driver is falling asleep, the technology alerts them to stop the car.

4) Choose one of the technologies above, or any other computer controlled systems in cars, planes or spacecraft. Research how technology has improved this mode of transport. Write about it here.

Mode of transport: _____

Type of technology: _____

How it makes this mode of transport safer: _____

61

13 Communicating in our region

TV signals

In the early days of television, the signals were sent using **analogue** technologies. The TV signal was carried by **wire** to **antennae**, which were mounted on a high place such as the top of a tall building. The antennae formed a **transmitter** that would **broadcast** the signal as an **electromagnetic wave** that could travel very long distances. A good signal could be received 100 km away from the antenna. You could have an **aerial** or **satellite dish** at your home to receive the signal. As the technology changed, digital signals replaced the analogue technology. This allowed better picture quality and more definition.

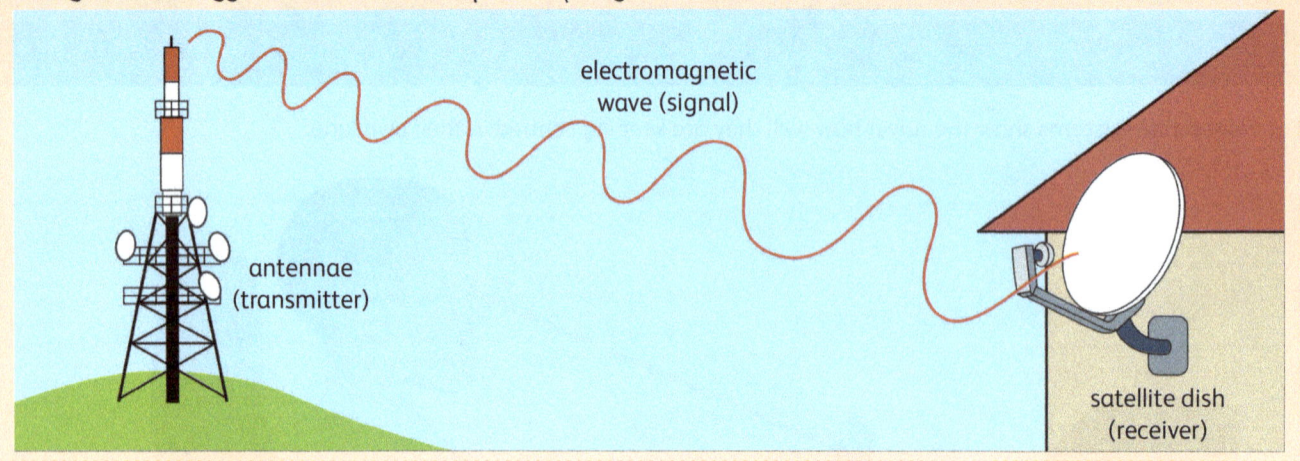

Which television signals do you receive in your country from other places in the Caribbean?
Write the names of different channels you can receive, and write which country they come from.

Name of channel	Country it comes from

62

Regional broadcasting

Sometimes in the Caribbean, special arrangements are made to broadcast regional events so that people throughout CARICOM or OECS countries can watch them. Examples of such events are conferences, meetings of the regional agencies and sports events.

20th Special Meeting of CARICOM Heads of Government: Opening Session, 3 July 2020

1. What does the picture show? _____

2. What do you notice about the way this meeting was held?

3. Why do you think it was important to hold this meeting remotely? (Hint: Look at the date. Think about what was happening in 2020.)

4. Why do you think this meeting needed to be broadcast to many countries in the region?

5. Think of a sporting event from another Caribbean country that you would like to see broadcast throughout the region. Write which one you would choose, and why you think it should be broadcast regionally.

63

Unit 13 Communicating in our region

Research

Which regional agencies promote news broadcasts on issues about the Caribbean?

Do some agencies hold video and audio meetings across countries?

1 Do some research to find out more about these questions. Discuss the questionnaire below with an adult. Share your results with others in your class.

    a Where do you usually read or hear about Caribbean news? For each item ticked, give more details below.

        ☐ Print media – names of newspapers or publications:
_____

        ☐ Local radio stations – names of radio stations or programmes:
_____

        ☐ International radio stations – names of radio stations or programmes:
_____

        ☐ News websites – names or URLs:
_____

        ☐ TV – names of channels/programmes:
_____

        ☐ Facebook – particular groups or channels:
_____

        ☐ Other – details:
_____

    b List the sites or platforms you use the most to get news about the Caribbean.
_____

2 Discuss the answers with others in your class. Which were the most popular sources of news information?
_____
_____

CaribVision

1 Read this information about CaribVision and answer the questions.

> CaribVision is a 24/7 cable channel owned and operated by the Caribbean Media Corporation (CMC). Launched in 2006, CaribVision now airs in over 22 Caribbean territories, the USA (New York Tri-State Area: New York, New Jersey and Connecticut) and the providences of Ontario and Quebec in Canada.
>
> With the chief objective of meeting the information and entertainment needs of Caribbean people and anyone with an enthusiasm for things Caribbean, CaribVision broadcasts a variety of culturally rich programming which includes news and current affairs, sports, drama, sitcoms, entertainment and lifestyle shows.
>
> (Source: caribvision.tv/about-us/)

a Who owns CaribVision? _____

b Do you get CaribVision transmissions in your country?

c Have you read or watched news reports on the site before?

2 Go to the caribvision.tv website. List three recent reports or shows under each category.

News	Entertainment	Sports	Talk or discussion

Revise and prepare

1. Communications such as mobile phone calls and emails are: (1)

    a transatlantic calls   b newscasts   c telecommunications

2. The first telephone call relied on technology that used: (1)

    a wires   b WiFi   c satellites

3. List five services, technologies or products that form part of 'The Internet of Things'. (5)

    _____

    _____

4. For each obstacle to communication, identify whether the cause is human or technological. (3)

    a short battery life in a mobile phone _____

    b lack of cellular signal _____

    c lack of information about local social media groups _____

5. A government decides to spend money laying fibre cables to each town and city, and allocates each parish some extra budget to cover free internet. This outcome will be to: (1)

    a create obstacles to communication

    b develop new technologies

    c remove obstacles to communication.

6. Identify and briefly describe four different technologies found in modern cars that use electronic communication systems to improve the safety of the vehicle. (4)

    _____

    _____

    _____

    _____

7. Draw a simple diagram to show how TV signals were broadcast using analogue technology. Show and label the transmitter, signal and receiver. (3)

8. Name two channels that might allow you to watch news or sports events across the Caribbean region. (2)

    _____   _____

(TOTAL: 20 marks)

14 Human resources

Education creates human resources

Human resources are resources that come from people. Our knowledge, skills, ideas, energy and labour all come from human resources.

Human resources develop through **education**. The very first skills a child learns are to feed, to recognise its parents, and later to lift its head and begin to crawl, walk, play and talk. This is **informal education** – we learn things by interacting with others and from our everyday experiences. However, usually when we talk about education, we are talking about **formal education**. Formal education takes place at different levels, as you can see in the diagram below.

1. Write some skills that people gain from education at each level. Some ideas have been filled in for you.

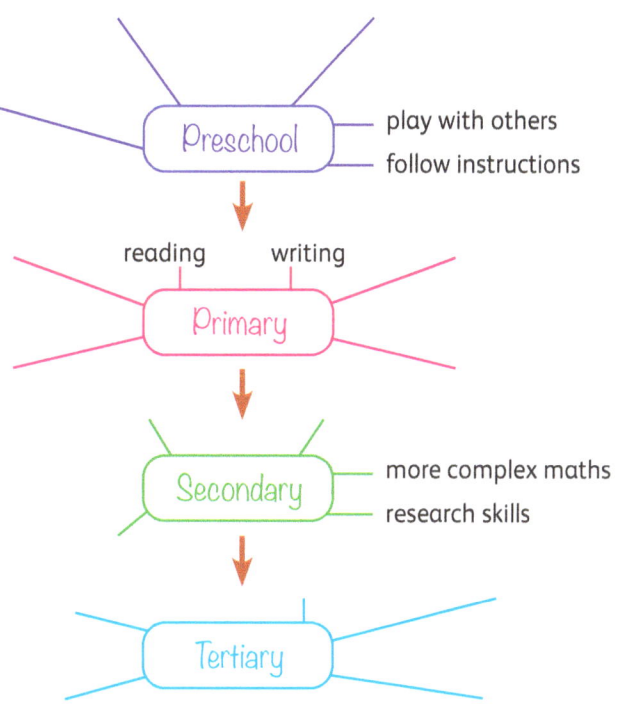

2. Why is it important for children to have free education at the primary level? Discuss with a partner and write your ideas here.

_____
_____
_____
_____
_____

67

Education in our country

A country can build up its human resources through **education**. Education is the process of developing knowledge and skills. You have learnt that children have the right to an education. For this reason, the government has a responsibility to provide schools throughout the country.

① Do some research to find out how many preschools, primary schools and secondary schools there are in your country. In the table below, write the total number of each type of school in your country. Write the names of five schools of each type.

Preschools	Primary schools	Secondary schools

② What do you think the consequence should be for a parent refusing to send their child to school?

_____
_____
_____

Special skills

For each picture, describe the special knowledge or skill the person has that allows them to do this job. What kind of special training or education do you think they need for this job?

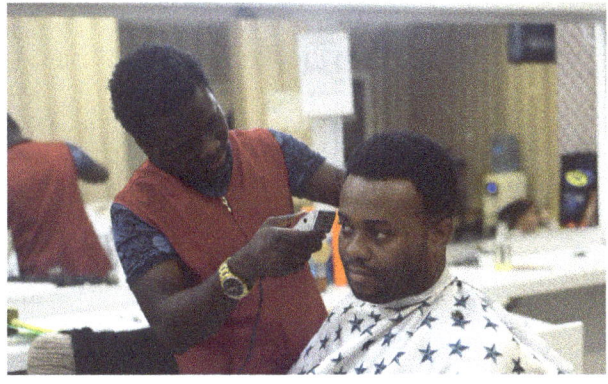

Unit 14 Human resources

The world of work

This career wheel divides the world of work into six broad areas. Around the wheel are some of the fields of work that fit into this area.

- event coordination
- art, music, dance and theatre
- entertainment
- radio and TV
- programming

- IT services
- software development
- graphic design
- journalism

- farming
- food technology
- conservation
- environmental science

- marine studies
- forestry
- sustainability

- medicine
- nursing
- laboratory services
- dental
- medical research

ARTS, TECHNOLOGY, INFORMATION SYSTEMS

AGRICULTURE, FOOD, NATURAL RESOURCES

HEALTH SCIENCES

BUSINESS, MARKETING AND MANAGEMENT

- finance
- banking
- tax services
- hospitality
- restaurants
- hotels

HUMAN SERVICES AND EDUCATION

SKILLED AND TECHNICAL SERVICES

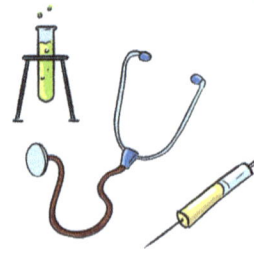

- teaching
- course coordination
- law
- social services
- emergency services

- civil service
- politics
- corrections and security

- architecture
- design
- construction
- science and technology
- transportation

- distribution and logistics
- trades (plumbing, carpentry)
- engineering

Colour the sector that interests you the most. Write a bit more below about the area you are interested in.

My favourite subjects at school are _____

My hobbies and personal interests include _____

I would be interested in the area of _____ because _____.

What I can picture myself doing when I am older: _____

15 Goods and services

Technical and Vocational Education and Training (TVET)

TVET stands for 'Technical and Vocational Education and Training'. TVET is a type of education aimed to give school-leavers specific skills in order to improve their ability to find employment. **Technical** courses may teach students how to use special technologies and practical skills that they need for their chosen field of work. They also teach **entrepreneurship** – the skills you need to start or run your own business. People who complete TVET courses have a greater chance of finding employment, and can contribute to the goods and services available in the country.

How do I know if TVET is right for me?
- Do you prefer to learn by doing?
- Do you like hands-on, practical work experience more than classroom learning?
- Do you have a specific field or career (vocation) in mind?
- Do you want to start working as soon as possible?
- Do you want to learn practical skills in a real-world environment?

If you answered yes to most of these questions, you may want to find out more about TVET. Contact your local TVET Council or college for more information!

❶ Below are some examples of TVET occupations. Shade any that look interesting to you.

baker	barber/ hairdresser	chef	travel agent	toolmaker	web designer	nail technician
interior designer	brickmason	plumber	fabric designer	firefighter	tailor	landscape designer
mechanic	appliance repairer	locksmith	paralegal	clothing designer	X-ray technician	dental hygienist
beauty therapist	carpenter	tour guide	welder	sound engineer	electrician	graphic designer

❷ Read the occupations in the blocks above. What are the main goods and/or services produced by persons employed in these occupations?

Goods: _____

Services: _____

71

Unit 15 Goods and services

Young people working

Read Catherine and Dan's stories. Then answer the questions.

> I grew up on a farm. I never thought of studying further until a counsellor spoke to me about a TVET course. She explained I could be an agricultural technician. I had never heard of that, but I know farming. Agricultural technicians help farmers. We maintain and repair agricultural facilities, equipment and tools. So now I understand machinery, and how to run a farm well. I can fix my own equipment. I can get a job at any farm, and I earn more than I could as a grower or picker.

> When I graduated with my school-leaving certificate, I had no job or training. I was interested in hairdressing, beauty therapy and nursing. I started studying nursing, and then I became more interested in medical technologies. I ended up working in a medical laboratory making prosthetics. I know there will always be a demand for my skills.

1   a   What areas of business appealed to Dan?
_____

    b   What areas appealed to Catherine?
_____

2   Suggest other areas of business that might be popular with young people.
_____

3   Governments see TVET as a way of reducing high unemployment among young people. Do you agree? Explain your answer.
_____
_____
_____

4   Look at the pictures. How does TVET improve the quality of products offered in your region?

_____
_____
_____

Improving goods and services through modern technology

Consumers are the people that buy and consume goods and services. Modern technology has changed the kind of service consumers enjoy. Many things are faster and more immediate. For example, you can book tickets for a sporting or cultural event on your own computer or telephone. We can pay bills from our own homes. We can send and receive messages in seconds.

Think about the different goods and services in the table. Give some examples of how consumers enjoy improved service as a result of modern technology.

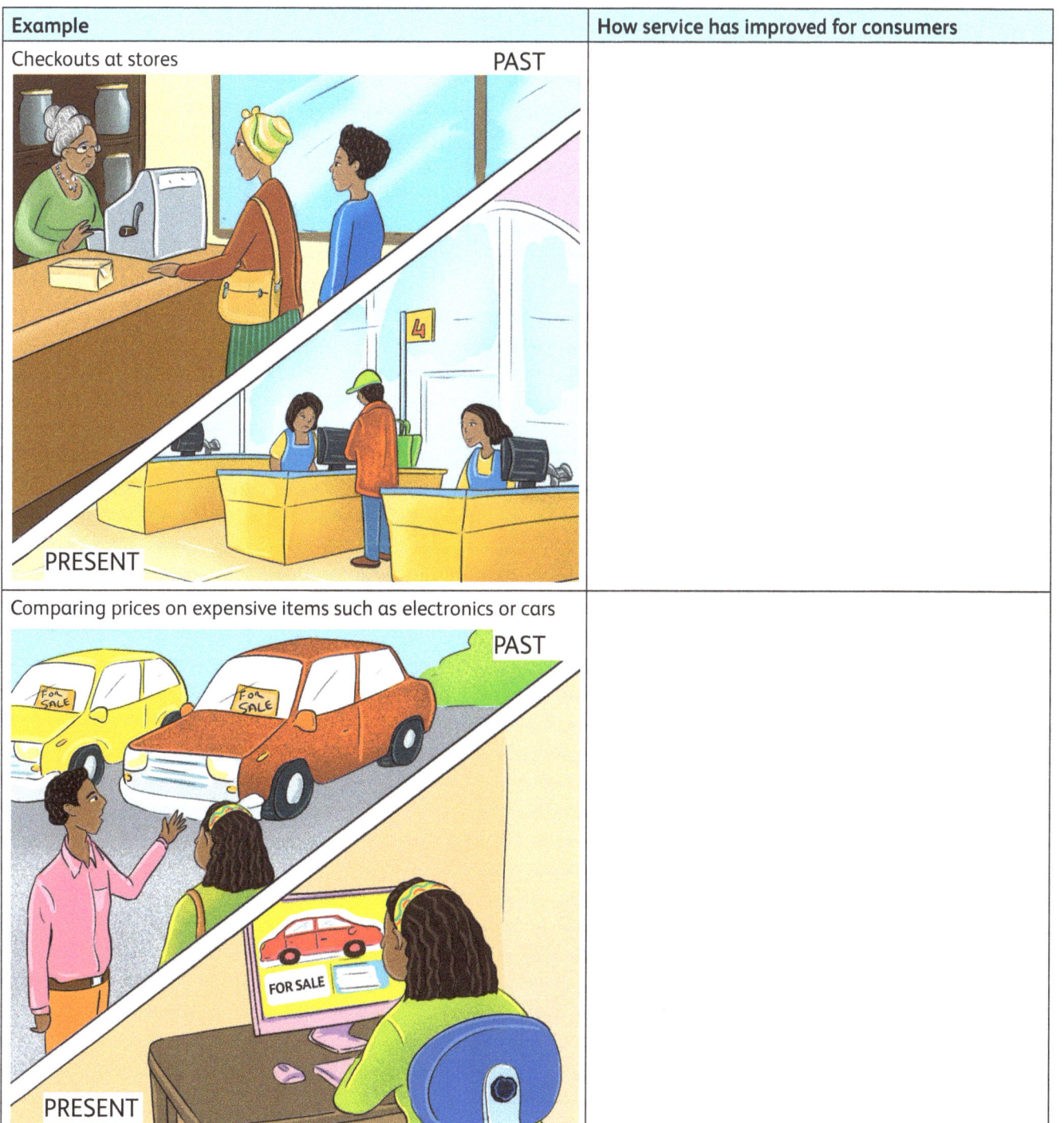

Example	How service has improved for consumers
Checkouts at stores (PAST / PRESENT)	
Comparing prices on expensive items such as electronics or cars (PAST / PRESENT)	

Unit 15 Goods and services

74

Science and technology in healthcare

Read the article. Then write definitions for the key words.

6 ways technology has improved healthcare

Technology has brought enormous changes to healthcare. Scientists have developed new cures, new treatments, new ways of caring for patients. The changes and improvements are continuous, but here are five areas that have seen enormous change.

1 Access to information

Not long ago, if you noticed unusual **symptoms**, you had to visit your local doctor for information. Today, you might type your symptoms into an online search, especially if your doctor is not immediately available. Sometimes you may find a simple explanation or remedy. Online information does not replace medical professionals, but it can help us to avoid panic and anxiety, or work out whether it is necessary to seek **medical advice**.

2 Online bookings, communications and results

Internet and email can make it easier to find a doctor, hospital or clinic. Many providers offer online bookings, and if you have a test or appointment, you may receive your results, **prescriptions** and bills by email instead of needing to travel to fetch them.

3 Treatments, equipment and medicine

Some life-threatening diseases have been largely wiped out because of the development of **vaccines** and treatments. New equipment allows doctors to treat patients more effectively. It also allows patients to manage their own health more easily. For example, people who suffer **chronic conditions** such as asthma or diabetes may use special equipment to help manage their condition so that it does not prevent them from living full, healthy lives.

Checking your own symptoms is easier than ever. Just be careful of misinformation!

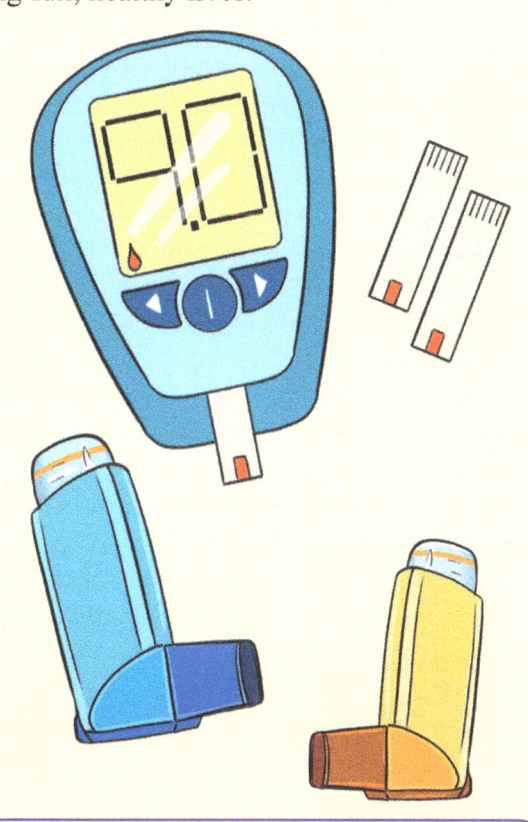

Diabetics may use blood glucose monitoring kits. Asthmatics may use inhalers. The technology for these systems has improved greatly in recent years.

75

4 Faster results and better records

In the past, people needed to wait days, weeks, or even months for their **medical test results**. Today, in many cases, there are tests with immediate results or results that come back within a day or two. Some hospitals and clinics may email your results or allow you to check them online yourself. Online systems may also allow patients to keep track of their appointments, prescriptions and bills.

5 Better record-keeping and patient relationships

Traditionally, doctors had to keep written notes in folders about each patient. If the patient moved areas or needed another doctor, the physical notes needed to be sent to that doctor's office. Technology allows doctors to keep their **medical records** in electronic form. This can be shared easily with the patient or with other professionals who need the records.

6 Improvements in data collection

When many people search for information about a particular illness, online search patterns quickly show researchers where **outbreaks** are happening. This can help the researchers to collect information about particular diseases and track outbreaks. The information may help health departments to respond quickly to outbreaks, and even prevent them from spreading.

key words

symptoms ....

....

medical advice ....

....

prescriptions ....

....

vaccine ....

....

chronic conditions ....

....

medical test results ....

....

medical records ....

....

outbreaks ....

....

Safety measures

> If you have not travelled by air, talk to someone who has in order to answer the questions. You could also do an internet search for 'airport safety procedures' to help you answer the questions.

1 There are many safety procedures at airports and other transportation points.

  a This security officer is scanning the bag for prohibited items – liquids, and sharp or flammable items. Why do you think these are prohibited on planes?

  b What is happening in the picture? How does this kind of scanner help keep passengers safe?

  c On board the plane, there is a safety card with instructions and diagrams. Explain what safety procedures are shown here.

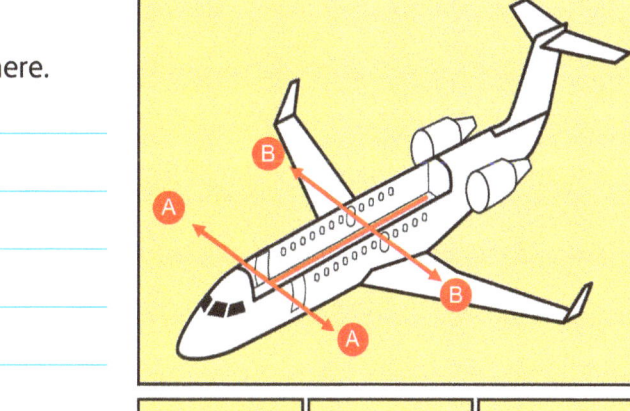

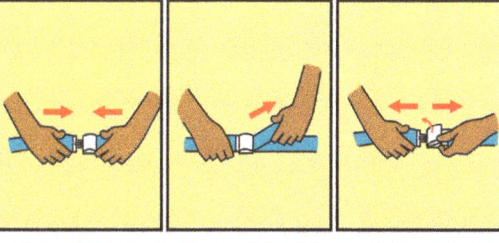

Revise and prepare

1. Human resources are: (1)
   a. natural resources that people use
   b. products that people make
   c. people who are skilled to provide goods and services

2. The best way to develop human resources is through: (1)
   a. environmental awareness
   b. education and training
   c. farming

3. Explain what we mean by primary, secondary and tertiary education. (3)

4. Explain what TVET stands for and give two reasons why it is important. (3)

5. Suggest three areas of business that young people may like to be employed in, and that would be suitable for TVET. (3)

6. Choose one of the following areas. Write a paragraph explaining at least four improvements that science and technology have made in this area. (4)
   - goods and services
   - healthcare
   - safety in transport.

(TOTAL: 15 marks)

16 Damage to the environment

Types of garbage

Materials we need to dispose of or throw away are known as **garbage**. We can classify our garbage in different ways. We may divide it into solid and liquid waste. Or we may classify it into recyclable and non-recyclable. Some of the different categories overlap.

1 Read about some of the different classifications for your garbage.

LIQUID WASTE – may be liquids from homes or from industry. Includes used and dirty water, organic liquids and chemicals, detergents and sewerage.

SOLID WASTE – all the solid materials that get thrown away by households and industry. This includes plastics, paper and card, tins and metals, ceramics and glass, as well as organic waste, which is anything that can rot or break down over time.

GREEN WASTE – landscaping and food waste that can decompose easily.

HAZARDOUS WASTE – anything flammable or toxic. This includes chemicals, paints, weedkillers and pesticides, household cleaners, and so on.

E-WASTE – electrical and electronic devices and parts. These may contain toxic metals that can be harmful to the environment.

RECYCLABLES – anything you can recycle, such as some kinds of plastic, glass, paper, tin and compostable organic wastes. Grey water (water from washing) is also recyclable.

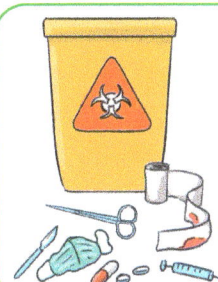

MEDICAL WASTE – used materials from clinics, hospitals and surgeries. Some may include equipment and packaging, such as used gloves, syringes or bandages. These items may contain used medicines, body fluids such as dried blood and traces of infectious diseases.

2 For each item, match it to three categories above.

a   a used bandage from your home   _____   _____   _____

b   an old, broken mobile phone   _____   _____   _____

c   paper cups from a hospital canteen   _____   _____   _____

79

Unit 16 Damage to the environment

Reasons for dumping

Why do so many individuals and companies dump their waste in streams, gullies and open land, instead of disposing of it at the proper sites?

1. Choose one of the reasons for dumping. Write your ideas for strategies that could help prevent people from dumping waste for this reason.

___

Dumped waste is not just unsightly and bad for the environment. It can also cause injury and disease. Some of the results of dumping are shown below.

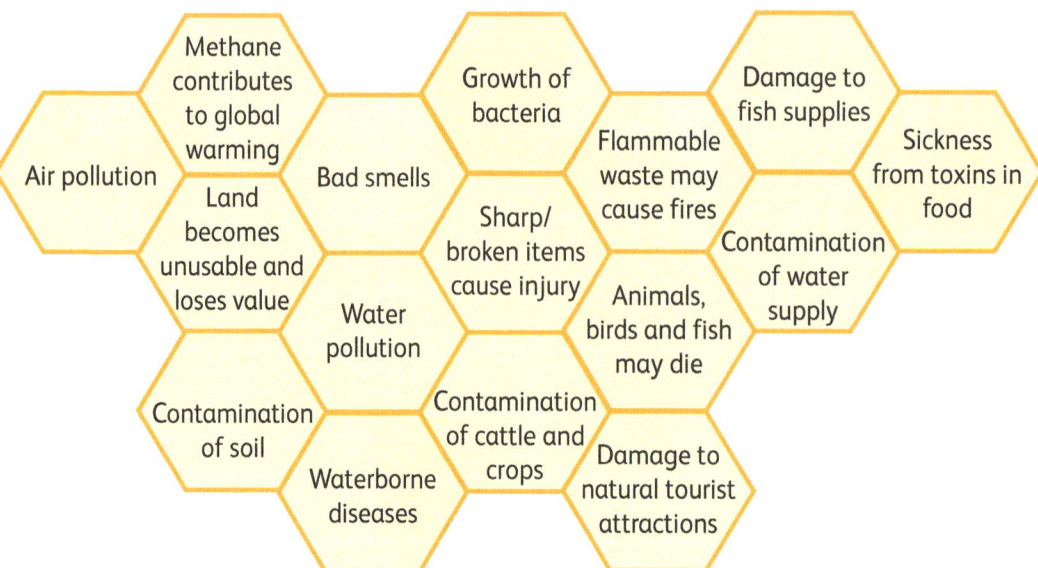

2. Use the ideas above to write a paragraph about the connection between dumping and its negative impact on your community.

___

80

17 Improving quality of life

Attitudes to our environment

1 Each statement expresses a cultural attitude. Does it harm or help the environment? Say why.

> I love buying new clothes as often as I can.

> I like having the latest device. I replace my phone each year.

> My community has regular gatherings where we clean our beach together.

_____
_____
_____

> In my family, our Christmas presents all need to be handmade from usable or recycled materials.

> My family enjoys flying to other islands for every holiday.

> My family buys takeaways twice a week. But instead of taking the disposable containers, we bring reusable boxes and cutlery.

_____
_____
_____

2 Design a poster that can raise awareness among younger students at your school to keep the environment litter-free.

3 A clean, healthy environment makes it more pleasant and appealing for us to go outside and be active. Write a song or poem that conveys this message.

Unit 17 Improving quality of life

Benefits of a healthy environment

Tourism is a very important part of the Caribbean economy. One of the main reasons that tourists visit the Caribbean is for the beautiful unspoilt natural attractions – the beaches, water activities, volcanoes, waterfalls and forests. If those environments are spoilt, they become unpleasant places to visit.

Draw pictures of four different places that tourists like to visit, which rely on an unspoilt or protected natural environment.

Revise and prepare

1. Plastic bottles from shampoo and shower gel are an example of: (3)
    a   household waste, solid waste and recyclable waste
    b   e-waste, household waste and liquid waste
    c   hazardous waste

2. List three reasons that people or companies dump waste illegally. (3)

3. A group of friends go for a picnic near the river. They leave many glass bottles and takeaway containers at the picnic site. Identify four ways this will negatively impact the environment. (4)

4. Explain what you understand by consumerism, and why this cultural attitude is harmful to the environment. (2)

5. Describe another cultural attitude or practice that harms the environment. Explain how it harms the environment, and suggest an alternative, or a way to help. (3)

(TOTAL: 15 marks)

CPEA Practice Questions

Family

1. If Sandy lives in a nuclear family, she lives with _____.

    a   her mum, dad and siblings

    b   her mum and siblings

    c   her grandparents, dad and cousins

2. Study the different types of families below, and identify the one that shows a single parent family.

Identity

1. Last summer, a group of History students travelled to study the Garifuna people. They visited _____.

    a   Dominica   b   Guyana   c   Belize

2. In the table below, which festival is correctly matched with the country where it is celebrated?

Country	Festival
a Barbados	John Canoe
b Grenada	Nine Mornings
c Jamaica	Crop Over
d Trinidad & Tobago	Diwali

3. Guadeloupe, Dominica, St. Lucia and Haiti all recognise _____ in the month of October to celebrate their French heritage.

    a   Hero's Day

    b   Carnival

    c   International Creole Day

4. Which statement is TRUE about our African ancestors?

    a   They travelled in canoes up the archipelago.

    b   They were explorers in search of gold, silk and spices.

    c   They were forced to work on plantations.

5. Which island is incorrectly matched to its capital city?
   a   Haiti – Port-au-Prince
   b   Dominica – Bridgetown
   c   Grenada – St. George's

6. The flag identifies the island of _____.
   a   Barbados
   b   St. Vincent and the Grenadines
   c   Grenada

7. Which public holiday reminds us of our ancestors' fight for freedom from enslavement?
   a   National Hero's Day
   b   Easter Sunday
   c   Emancipation Day

8. Which of these practices was passed down from our European ancestors?
   a   making wooden canoes
   b   worshipping a Christian God
   c   telling Anansi stories

9. During a Social Studies class, Mrs Jones asked the students to give examples that explain the ideal Caribbean person. Which student gave the least appropriate answer?

   a   Shania (demonstrating national pride)
   b   Sunita (being responsible)
   c   Jacob (teasing children who are different from me)

10. The Caribbean people are most alike because they _____.
    a   enjoy travelling
    b   share a common history
    c   all speak English

11. Sherice is studying cultural celebrations unique to Caribbean people. She would therefore be interested in learning more about all of these EXCEPT:

   a   Carnival

   b   Jounen Kweyol

   c   Halloween

Location

1. In which direction will one travel from E.T. Joshua Airport to get to Piarco International Airport?

   a   westerly

   b   southerly

   c   northerly

2. The Caribbean island which is completely surrounded by the Atlantic Ocean is _____.

   a   Barbados

   b   St. Lucia

   c   Dominica

3. Which statements are TRUE about the line marked X below?

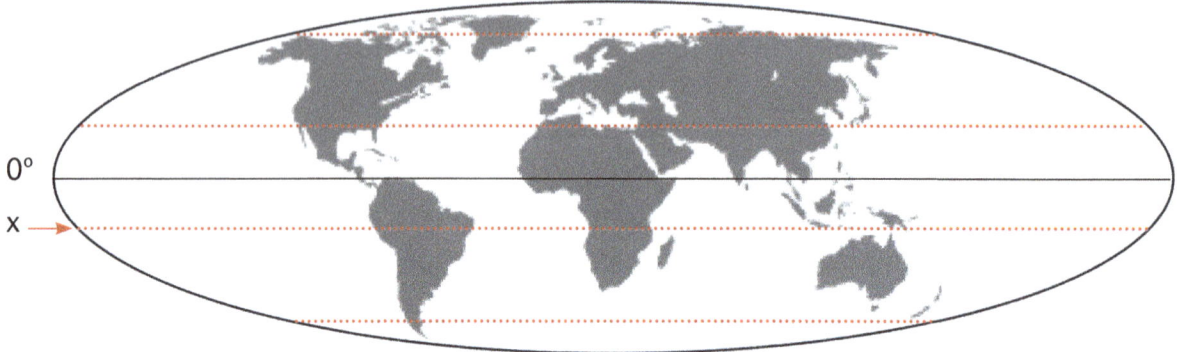

   i.   It is called the Tropic of Capricorn.
   ii. It is a line of latitude.
   iii. It is north of the Equator.
   iv. It has a value of 23 ½°S.

   a   i, ii, iii

   b   i, ii, iv

   c   i, iii, iv

Study the statement below. Answer Questions 4, 5, 6 and 7.

> Mark lives at Country A but spends his school holidays with his uncle in Country B.

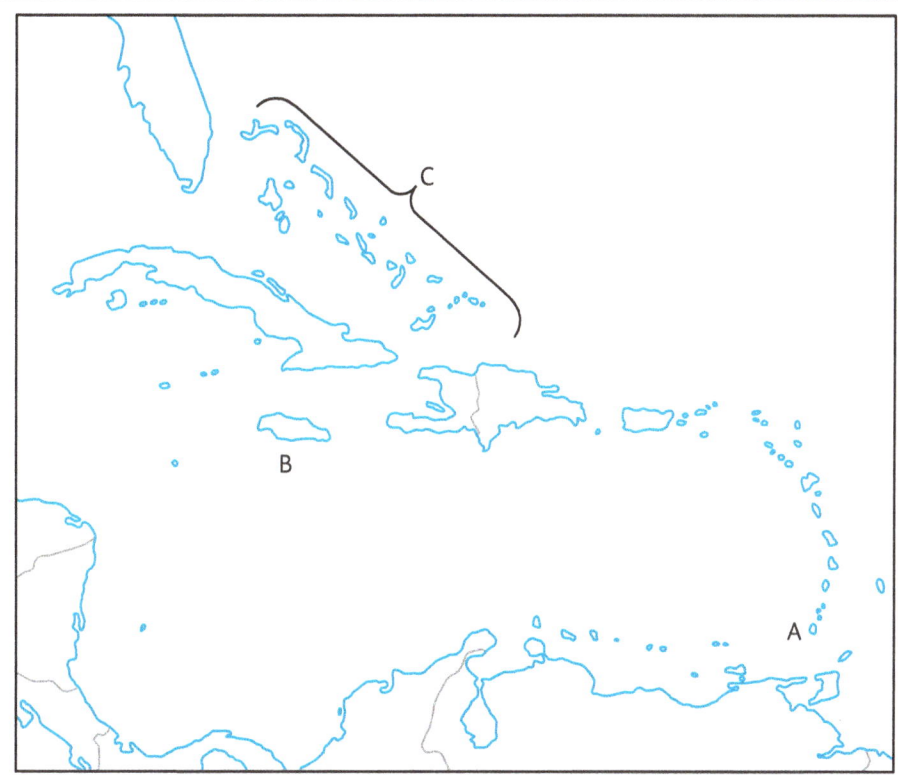

4 Country B is called _____.

    a   Cuba

    b   Haiti

    c   Jamaica

5 The people in Country A mostly speak _____.

    a   English

    b   French

    c   Spanish

6 While in country B, Mark can _____.

    a   visit the Caroni Swamp

    b   explore Harrison's Cave

    c   climb the Blue Mountains

7 The group of islands labelled C is called the _____.

    a   Windward Islands

    b   Greater Antilles

    c   Bahamas

Use the map below to answer Questions 8 to 11.

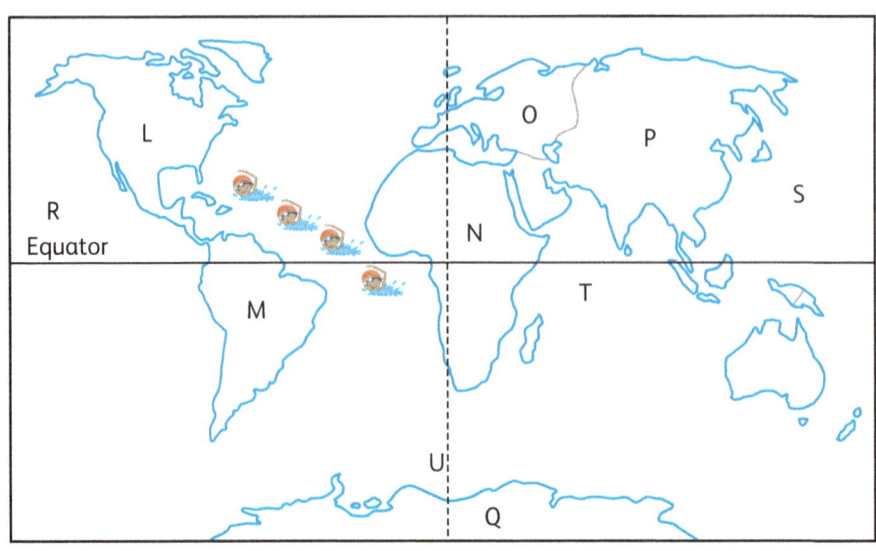

8. While visiting Continent M, Joe could _____.

   a   travel down the Amazon River

   b   explore the Rocky Mountains

   c   ride a camel across the Sahara Desert

9. Which pair is correctly matched?

   a   L = North America

   b   Q = Australia

   c   N = Asia

10. Max is swimming from N to St. Lucia. Which ocean is he most likely crossing?

    a   Atlantic Ocean

    b   Pacific Ocean

    c   Southern Ocean

11. The continent labelled O is located _____.

    a   east of Asia

    b   north of Africa

    c   in the western hemisphere

Government

1. All of these people can cast a ballot at the next general election in my country EXCEPT _____.

   a   Josie, an eighteen year old student

   b   Mike, who is currently in prison

   c   Miss Mary, the manager at KFC

88

② This organisation was formed after the Second World War to ensure World Peace. Which of these organisations is it?

   a   OECS

   b   UN

   c   OAS

③ All of these islands are members of the OECS EXCEPT _____.

   a   St. Lucia

   b   Barbados

   c   St. Vincent and the Grenadines

④ Which island below has a president as a Head of State?

   a   St. Lucia

   b   Jamaica

   c   Dominica

⑤ WHO is an organisation that provides aid in the area of _____.

   a   hotel management

   b   climate change

   c   health

⑥ Which of these is a republic?

   a   Trinidad & Tobago

   b   Barbados

   c   Antigua

⑦ Which of the following is responsible for making government policies?

   a   Cabinet

   b   Senate

   c   Parliament

⑧ This speech is delivered by the Governor General every year before the formal debate of the National Budget:

   a   Estimates of Expenditures

   b   Prime Minister's Address

   c   Throne Speech

9 What do these islands have in common?

Montserrat, St. Lucia, Grenada, Antigua

    a   They are all independent nations

    b   They all use the EC currency

    c   They are all Leeward Islands

Constitution

1 Read each statement below. All of these are rights of a child EXCEPT _____.

    a   Right to a name

    b   Right to be educated

    c   Right to marriage

2 Jamie was arrested for demonstrating outside parliament. To find out what his right is in this situation he should consult the _____.

    a   Bible

    b   Constitution

    c   newspaper

Organisations

1 Which of these regional organisations are matched to the correct acronyms?

i. Caribbean Public Health Agency	ii. Caribbean Development Bank	iii. Caribbean Court of Justice
CARPHA	CARICOM	CCJ

    a   i, ii

    b   i, iii

    c   i, ii, iii

2 Which of the following statements about CARICOM are TRUE?

    i.   It is made up of all countries in and around the Caribbean Sea.

    ii.   It helps trade and economic development in member states.

    iii.   It speaks with a united voice on world issues.

    iv.   It created the CSME.

        a   i, iii, iv

        b   i, ii, iii

        c   i, ii, iii, iv

3. Fill in the blanks in the paragraph below. Choose the answer which has the missing words in the correct sequence.

The Organisation of Eastern Caribbean States also called the _____, has _____ Caribbean territories which have come together to achieve _____ and unity. Its currency, the EC dollar is issued by the Eastern Caribbean Central Bank based in _____ and _____.

   a OECS, eleven, St. Kitts, political, Nevis
   b OECS, eleven, cooperation, St. Kitts, Nevis
   c cooperation, OECS, eleven, Nevis, St. Kitts.

4. The Queen of England visited the Caribbean on her tour of the Commonwealth. Which of the following statements about the Commonwealth is NOT TRUE?

   a The Commonwealth is only made up of Caribbean countries.
   b Independent countries from around the world make up the Commonwealth.
   c Caribbean countries which are members take part in the Commonwealth Games.

Use the pictures below to answer Questions 5 to 7.

i.   ii.   iii.

5. What are the names of these documents?

   a i Identification card; ii Birth certificate; iii Passport
   b i Passport; ii Identification card; iii Birth certificate
   c i Passport; ii Birth certificate; iii Identification card

6. What can ALL of these documents be used for?

   a Identifying a citizen of a country
   b Registering a child at a school in a foreign country
   c Travelling to foreign countries.

7. Your father wants to take you on a holiday to another Caribbean country. Since you are under 16 years old, he will need to have you included on his passport. Which documents should he take to the Immigration Office to have this done?

   a His Identification card, his Passport, his Birth certificate
   b Your Identification card, his Passport, your Birth certificate
   c His Identification card, his Passport, your Birth certificate

Social issues

1. Mr Yatali started to use illegal drugs. He then could not do his job properly. His boss told him to get help or he would fire him. Which person is the best one to help him?

    a   Mr Stern, the village policeman

    b   Mrs Alert, a psychologist

    c   Mr Arnold, his son's teacher

2. Which social issues and pictures are correctly matched?

    i.   Covid 19 safety   ii.   Poverty   iii.   Alcoholism   iv.   Bullying

    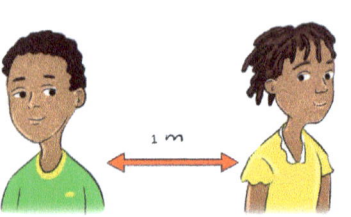   

    a   i, ii

    b   i, iii, iv

    c   i, iv

3. Wendy has an elderly neighbour, Miss Janice, who lives alone. Wendy shows caring by

    a   chatting with Miss Janice every day

    b   refusing to help Miss Janice when she asks for help

    c   picking Miss Janice's mangoes without permission

Trade, Industry, Resources

Study the illustration below, then answer Questions 1 to 3.

1. The raw material used to make this chocolate bar is _____.

    a   oil

    b   ginger

    c   cocoa

2. The primary worker employed in the chocolate industry most likely _____.
   a   sold the chocolate bars
   b   grew and harvested the cocoa pods
   c   processed the cocoa to make chocolate

3. A country's most valuable resource is human beings because _____.
   a   they use resources only for themselves
   b   they can identify resources and use them wisely
   c   they exploit and cause resources to become extinct

Use the table below to answer Questions 4 and 5.

Country	Imports	Exports
St. Lucia	$453 698 914	$403 906 000
Trinidad & Tobago	$404 596 830	$407 000 000
Guyana	$98 653 712	$106 458 123
St. Vincent and the Grenadines	$92 985 461	$93 002 879

4. Which of the following countries experienced a trade deficit?
   a   St. Lucia
   b   Trinidad & Tobago
   c   Guyana

5. Some of the money made from exports in Trinidad & Tobago most likely came from the sales of _____.
   a   bauxite
   b   petroleum
   c   lumber

Study the information below. Answer Questions 6 to 8.

Antigua imports cars from Japan

6. The above statement is an example of _____ trade.
   a   local
   b   regional
   c   international

93

7. The government of Antigua would most likely pay the Japanese car company in _____.
   a   Yen
   b   Pounds
   c   Pesos

8. The best way to transport cars from Japan to Antigua is by _____.
   a   airplane
   b   cargo ship
   c   train

9. Conservation of forests in the Windward Islands is mainly _____.
   a   for tourists to explore
   b   to protect the water supply
   c   to create employment

10. All of these are direct reasons for trade EXCEPT _____.
    a   to sell surplus goods to other countries
    b   to generate foreign revenue
    c   to provide for our social needs

11. Which flow chart represents the production process?
    a   producer ⟶ wholesaler ⟶ retailer ⟶ consumer
    b   producer ⟶ retailer ⟶ wholesaler ⟶ consumer
    c   consumer ⟶ retailer ⟶ producer ⟶ wholesaler

12. Lewis wants to set up a factory to make coconut confectioneries. Which list below contains what is necessary for production to take place?
    a   air, land, water
    b   food, clothing, shelter
    c   land, labour, capital

13. This list contains ONLY renewable resources.
    a   bauxite, petroleum, gold
    b   animals, gold, natural gas
    c   humans, plants, water

Tourism

1 Tourism does all of the following EXCEPT:

　a　encourages tourists to visit Caribbean beaches

　b　brings in foreign exchange

　c　creates year-round jobs

2 The BEST ways to attract tourists from outside of the Caribbean is:

　a　put advertisements on travel websites

　b　do radio advertisements

　c　put up huge billboards in each Caribbean country

Environmental issues

1 John and Esther wrote sentences on pollution for a project on World Environment Day. Which of their sentences are TRUE?

　i.　Air pollution is caused by carbon dioxide and oxygen.

　ii.　Water pollution is caused by the dumping of garbage and harmful chemicals in rivers.

　iii.　Global warming can cause the sea level to fall.

　iv.　Pollution can be slowed down by using less oil and coal for fuel.

　　a　i, ii, iv

　　b　ii, iii, iv

　　c　ii, iv.

Use the pictures below to answer Questions 2 to 4 on the next page.

2 From the table below, choose the statement which shows the correct environmental actions under each heading.

	Polluting activities	Non-polluting activities
a	Clearing trees to build factories	Planting trees
b	Releasing factory waste into the sea	Using fossil fuels
c	Using energy from the wind	Using solar panels to produce energy

3 Many world countries have agreed to work towards keeping the world temperature to below 2 degrees Celsius by _____.

   a   increasing use of coal and gas in manufacturing industries

   b   replanting forests

   c   reducing the ozone layer

4 Industries and forests are BOTH useful to _____.

   a   meet our needs for food, clothing and shelter

   b   maintain a healthy environment

   c   provide jobs for large numbers of people